Talk Like a Pirate!

Over 450 words!

Pirate words, phrases,
history, and character tips.
by Lady Wench and Grace O'Blarney

Cover graphic, Pirate Idea, © Cory Thoman / http://www.900foot.com/
courtesy of Dreamstime.com

Any trademarks, service marks, or product names are assumed to be the property of their respective owners, and are used only for general reference.

Important aspects of any activity can change without notice. Therefore, our experiences may not be typical, and our information may not seem accurate -- or be current -- when you're reading this book. Then again, it might be due to a shift from one reality to a parallel one. These things happen. Go with the flow. Arrr!

DISCLAIMER

This information in book is provided as entertainment. We have done everything possible and reasonable to assure accuracy in our research and writing. Information is based on personal experience and anecdotal reports, and should not replace legal, medical, religious or other professional advice, including that from time travelers who've encountered real pirates in this or other dimensions. Readers assume full responsibility for use of the information in this book.

New Forest Books™
PO Box 2216
Concord, New Hampshire 03302-2216 USA

www.NewForestBooks.com

Table of Contents

Introduction

Ahoy, me hearties!

Okay... I don't *really* talk like that when I write, though it *is* fun, especially on Talk Like a Pirate Day (September 19th).

The real pirate world? Like many pirate enthusiasts, I've studied real pirate history (it's in this book), and I've also created my own version. It's more real to me than anything written by people who take reality just a little too seriously.

Sure, there's a real history in my pirate world, and it's mostly from the 18th century. Pirate enthusiasts like me have embellished that with romance and a lot of imagination.

That's what this book is about: Facts and fun combined with real history and authentic words.

In *Talk Like a Pirate,* you'll learn the basics of talking like a pirate. You can learn to talk like a pirate in five minutes, if you just need a few good words.

We've added an extensive pirate dictionary with about 500 genuine pirate, maritime, and nautical words so you'll sound authentic... and know what you're saying. I've woven plenty of fascinating trivia throughout, as well.

You'll also discover the real history of pirates, with tips for choosing a pirate persona and then dressing the part.

And, you'll pick up some great trivia and tips if you choose to talk (and act) like a pirate for a day... or every day.

I'm Grace O'Blarney (not my real name, of course), and my daughter is Lady Wench (not her real name, either). I did most of the research and writing based on her ideas and input. Both of us grew up being dazzled by attractions like Disney's Pirates of the Caribbean.

Today, we've carried those fantasies forward and it's become... well, more than a hobby. At times, especially at events like Dragon*Con, *it's a way of life.*

Author Frank Stockton said it well when he described childhood images of piracy.

"They know that pirates are wicked men, that, in fact, they are sea-robbers or maritime murderers, but their bold and adventurous method of life, their bravery, daring, and the exciting character of their expeditions, give them something of the same charm and interest which belong to the robber knights of the middle ages.

"The one mounts his mailed steed and clanks his long sword against his iron stirrup, riding forth into the world with a feeling that he can do anything that pleases him, if he finds himself strong enough.

"The other springs into his rakish craft, spreads his sails to the wind, and dashes over the sparkling main with a feeling that he can do anything he pleases, provided he be strong enough."

I think many of us imagine pirates as a combination of King Arthur's knights of the Round Table, romantic highwayman, and Robin Hood... but on the open seas, facing challenges from both man and nature with raucous humor and a heart of gold.

That's the version of piracy that has sparked tremendous popularity, and a subculture that embraces all things related to pirates: Their senses of style and humor, and everything related to Talk Like a Pirate Day.

Welcome to Talk Like a Pirate! My daughter and I hope you enjoy this book.

Sincerely,

Grace O'Blarney

Grace O'Blarney
Grace@TalkLikeAPirate.org
P.S. Our website is http://TalkLikeAPirate.org

Basic Pirate Slang
(Quick-Start Guide)

Speaking to landlubbers:

If you need to sound like a pirate for Talk Like a Pirate Day (September 19th) or a party, just a few pirate-y words or pirate phrases can be enough.

With a pirate's hat or a scarf tied round your head (like Johnny Depp as Jack Sparrow), a fake parrot on your shoulder, and adding extended Rs to your speech – Arr! – you might be all set. It depends on the party.

The founders of Talk Like a Pirate Day, Mark Summers (Cap'n Slappy) and John Baur (Ol' Chumbucket), have said that you only need five pirate words to pass muster, and all of them begin with the letter A:

Ahoy! (Hello!)
Avast! (Stop! Wait!)
Aye! (Yes!)
Aye, aye! (I heard what you said and I'll take care of it.)
Arr! (Yes, uh-huh, gotcha, or just a vague agreement. In fact, extending almost any worrrd with an R in it can earrrn you extrrra points.)

In our opinion, adding the occasional "Shiver me timbers!" can't hurt, and you'll get bonus points for telling a woman she's a right smart beauty. ("Right" is an all-purpose adjective, and "smart" means sharp. "Beauty" is exactly what it sounds like.)

At the next level of pirate talk, you'll swap "ye" for "you" and change many of your passive verbs to "be." Shift everything to the present tense, if you can. In other words, ye'll be sounding more pirate-like, right quickly. (Trust us, it's easy to fall into this way of talking, once you relax. Or have a cup of grog. Or both.)

Cadence helps. In other words, get the rhythm right and you're halfway there.

You know the rhythm of the words when someone tries to fake an Irish accent and say, "Top o' the mornin' to ya"? Well, lose the Irish accent (maybe) but keep that rhythm. It's not quite sing-song-y, but it can get pretty close.

(Don't overdo it, of course. If you slip and say something that sounds *truly* awful or stupid, pause, rub your jaw, and mutter, "Arrr!" thoughtfully. It's not a perfect save, but it can work. If you're a woman and you're wearing garb, pause and adjust your bodice. That usually diverts attention from any blunder.)

Next, replace the word "my" with "me," and exaggerate when you can. So, instead of saying "That's my car," you'll say, "That's me conveyance." (Don't attempt "That be me conveyance" unless you can get the accent and cadence just right.)

Double your adjectives. Never use one when you can use two. (Don't extend it to three adjectives. That'd sound silly.)

As already suggested, "right" can be thrown into almost any phrase, meaning something that's true or real. "Grand" is another useful adjective, for anything big, good, or impressive.

So, your partner's grin is a "right grand smile," and your beverage is a "right grand drink."

Drop or slur letters whenever possible, such as saying "cap'n" instead of "captain."

The letter G is the easiest to lose when it's on the end of any word. *Ye be visitin'* wherever you are, for example. If someone says something to offend you, or you can pretend you're offended, you'll say, "Them be fightin' words."

For the rest of ye aspirin' pirates:

This be the list of words ye need, when all y'need is to make a pirate-y impression.

(If ye be wantin' more scuttlebutt, see what th' cap'n has fer ye in th' Pirate Dictionary. A right quick glance at the Table of Contents'll lead ye thar.)

Ahoy!

> A call (or shout) used to draw attention. A way of greeting pirates since 1751, and maybe earlier.

Arr, Harr, Yarr (and other variations)

> Yeah, yes, or a muttered (reluctant) agreement. An all-purpose comment or reply.

Avast

> Stop!

Aye

Yes. (Said twice – "Aye, aye!" -- to an order:
Once to say you heard it, and once to say you'll
follow-through.)

Batten down

Secure whatever-it-is. Get ready for trouble.

Be

Replaces almost all forms of "to be," including is,
am, are, was, were, will be, and so on.

Beauty

A woman, often a lovely one. Also used to
describe anything appealing or coveted.

Black spot

A circular piece of cut paper or card, all black on
one side and sometimes with a message on the
other side. It means guilty, condemned, or – in
the case of a captain – deposed.

Blast!

An expletive meaning hatred or extreme
annoyance. (Also: Blast it! Blast it all! Blasted
_____!)

Blunt

Money, especially coins.

Booty

> Treasure or plunder taken by thieves.

Broadside

> Fire all the artillery – guns and cannons -- on one side of a ship, all at once.

Buccaneer

> A pirate, originally those who roved and plundered the Spanish Main in the 17th century.

Cape Horn fever

> A false illness claimed by someone who only wants to avoid work.

Careen

> Turn the boat or ship upside down to scrape it clean of seaweed and barnacles, and make repairs. Radically clean whatever-it-is.

Cat o' nine tails

> A disciplinary whip made by separating nine strands of a rope. Also called the "cap'n's daughter."

Crimp

> A swindler or a cheat.

Cur

A mongrel dog or an unworthy person.

Davy Jones' Locker

The bottom of the ocean, or the grave of those who perish at sea.

Dead men

Empty bottles, or sometimes empty casks, because (a pun) the "spirit" has left.

Deep six

To get rid of something or someone, usually by throwing overboard. (A fathom is about six feet, so a deep six is more than that.)

Doubloons

A Spanish gold coin equal to 128 reales, or 16 pieces of eight.

Even keel

When the keel of the ship is parallel to the horizon.

Fathom

As a noun, it's a measure of about six feet. As a verb, it's to get the measure of someone or a situation.

Fiddler's Green

> The personal heaven of pirates, with plenty of wine, women and song.

Flash in the pan

> Anything of short duration, especially something that started with great promise. When gunpowder in a flintlock's priming pan is ignited, but it doesn't set off the charge.

Fouled

> Spoiled, jammed, tangled, ruined, or otherwise made unusable.

French leave

> When a sailor leaves his post (or, usually, the ship) – with or without permission – intending to return, preferably without his absence being noticed.

Furner

> One who cooks bread in his own oven. Extended to mean a ship purchased (not stolen) by its captain.
>
> (Or, the word "foreigner" could sound like that.)

Galley

> In early times, it was a large warship manned with banks of oars. In the pirate realm, it's more often the kitchen or hearth where food is cooked on the ship.

Gangway!

> Clear a path!

Gentleman o' fortune

> Euphemism meaning a pirate.

Go on the account, Going on account

> When someone quit the Royal Navy and took to the high seas as a pirate. Anyone who signed on as a pirate. Also, a phrase a captain used when planning an expedition, and looking for volunteers.

Grog

> Weak spirits, usually rum diluted with water. (For this recipe and more, see the Pirates Dictionary section of this book.)

Half-cocked

> Keeping your flintlock partially cocked so it's ready to fire on short notice. Figuratively, someone who's wound up; an outburst is imminent.

Hazard, Hazzard

> Since the 16th century, a game of chance
> involving two dice and rules that vary widely,
> often changed on the fly. Likewise, to put
> something at risk, as in a game of chance.

Hearties

> A brave man of the sea. Those with heart and
> those who remain loyal.

Heave ahead

> To pull the boat or ship forward by pulling on the
> rope or chain attached to the anchor. (The anchor
> will be somewhere astern the ship, usually a short
> distance ahead.)
>
> (Heave astern = backwards; Heave to = stop.)

Hornswoggler, Hornswaggler

> A 19th-century term meaning anyone who cheats,
> lies, or swindles others.

Jack

> A small flag, usually smaller than the ensign. On
> a ship, usually a small flag identifying nationality.
> Flown from the jack-staff at the bow of the ship.
> Or, the word can mean a sailor.

Jolly Roger

> The pirate's flag.

Keelhaul

Punishment usually resulting in death by tying the condemned to a rope and dragging him along the barnacle-covered hull of the ship.

Landlubber

Anyone who doesn't meet the basic requirements of a pirate, usually someone who's new to the sea. (A "lubber" is someone clumsy who doesn't work and doesn't pull his own weight, no matter where he is.)

Lass

An unmarried woman, usually a girl.

Letting the cat out of the bag

Betraying a trust or giving out secrets.
Punishment usually meant a flogging, signaled by taking the cat o' nine tails out of its storage bag.

Lily-livered

Someone with no courage.

Loaded to the Gunwales (said like, "Gunnels")

Drunk.

Make land

To spot (or see) land from the ship, and usually to head towards it with the intention of dropping anchor.

Matey

> Shipmate.

Me

> My or mine. Example: Me hearties, meaning my
> loyal friends. (Like the word "the" replaced by
> "th'," there are times when you'll replace "my"
> with just "m'," said like "muh.")

Mizzenmast

> On a three-masted ship, the mast at the rear.

Motley crew

> A mismatched crew, often dressed very
> differently. (A pirate's style of dress usually
> revealed where he was from.)

No quarter given

> When an enemy who surrenders is spared death,
> but that's the limit of the pirates' generosity.
> Resistance of any kind means immediate death.

Pieces o' eight

> A Spanish coin that was worth eight reales, and it
> could be cut into pieces (up to eight) as smaller
> denominations. Today, slang for coins.

Powder monkey

> The boy or sailor who supplies powder to the gunners. Today, slang for anyone procuring provisions like food or drink.

Press gang

> Wharf laborers whose job was to recruit sailors by any means, usually by force or by getting them drunk.

Privateer

> A sailor or ship captain with a contract (Letter of Marque) from a government, authorizing him or her to attack enemy ships, and share the plunder with the authorizing government.

Purser rigged and parish damned

> Describes a man who went to sea to escape troubles – legal or marital – on land.

Run a rig

> To run a scam, play a trick, or deliberately fool someone.

Savvy

> To understand. (As a question, it's usually just, "Savvy...?") From the French word, savoir, to know, to taste (often, figuratively), or to understand.

Scallywag, Scallawag, Scalliwag

> A scoundrel, disreputable fellow or mischief-maker. (In pirate circles, that can be a compliment.)

Scuttlebutt

> Gossip, tales, or rumors. Water was stored in a butt (a cask) and it was scuttled (a hole bored in it) so people could get drinking water. So, this was the pirate version of conversation around the water cooler.

Skedaddle

> To slip quietly away from a fight or a battle, without giving notice to your party.

Sprog

> A child or lively young man, usually a raw recruit.

Squadron

> A relatively small detachment of soldiers or a few warships (ten or less). Usually said in a derogatory, "you've got to be kidding" tone.

Squiffy

> 19th century expression for drunk.

Swab, Swabber

A swab is a sort of long mop, often made from strands of rope and a stick, used for cleaning the ship's decks. A swabber – sometimes just "a swab" is the person whose job it is to clean the deck. (A sea-swabber is someone lazy who does nothing of use.)

Swaggy

Describes an enemy's ship that's filled with plunder. Usually, an intended target.

Swashbuckling

Fighting on the high seas. To "swashbuckle" is to strike an enemy's shield with your sword.

Sweet trade

Another name for a pirate's work, but especially that of a buccaneer.

Th'

Replaces the word "the" when you can slur the words together or say it so it's not far removed from "duh"... except not in a stupid way. At other times, when it punctuates or adds flair to your speech, you'll say "the" like "thee," so it has a sharp punch to it.

"Th' lady" can be an aside or said with a touch of reverence, but – in other situations -- "the lady," said with a good stretch sounding like "thee lay-dee," it has the right sarcastic edge to it.

Thar

> There, indicating location.

Them

> Sometimes used instead of "they" or "those."
> Usually used with singular verbs ("them is," etc.).
> Example: "Them's jus' swabbies, mateys. Leave
> 'em be." Or, "Them be right fine jewels yer
> sportin', ma'am, an' prolly a might bit heavy on
> ye, too."

Walk the plank

> When a prisoner on a ship was forced to walk,
> bound and blindfolded, along a board that
> extended outward from the deck of the ship. In
> most cases, the person fell into the sea and
> drowned.

Wench

> A female, usually a young woman. Attractive but
> approachable.

Wi' a wannion, With a wannion (waniron, wenion)

> 16th century phrase, perhaps older, meaning with
> a vengeance.

Ye

> You. Always pepper your pirate talk with "ye"
> instead of "you," and salt it with a few "arrs."

Yo-ho-ho

>A pirate's laugh.

Assorted expressions of surprise, annoyance, etc.

Blimey!

>Surprise, short for "gorblimey" or "God blind me."

By the Powers!

>Surprise, uttered by Long John Silver.

Scurvy dog!

>Insult, meaning someone who's low, mean, and unworthy.

Shiver me timbers!

>Surprise, usually leaving the person otherwise speechless.

Sink me!

>Amazement, short for "Sink me to the Devil!"

Pirate Dictionary

This be the
right grand expanded version of what were afore. Ye'll
find a good 500 pirate, nautical, and maritime words
here.

(If ye be a landlubber seekin' a few right choice words,
skedaddle back to the Pirate Slang pages, an' look lively
about it. Yarr!)

The words are organized, ship-shape an' Bristol fashion,
in alphabetical orderrr. If'n we missed any right
important words, visit TalkLikeAPirate.org and let us
know.

A

Abaft

> Towards the back, rear, or stern of the boat, or
> anything that – relative to another object – is
> farther back. Often just "aft." Related: Abaft the
> beam means more than 90 degrees in back of the
> beam, usually referencing the bow of the ship.

Abandon Ship

> Leave the ship immediately, usually in the face of
> extreme danger. Leave a sinking ship, or quit
> something that's failing.

According to Robin Miskolcze, author of Women and Children First: 19th-Century Sea Narratives and American Identity, the English (including those in the Americas) – of the mid-1700s and earlier -- believed that surviving a shipwreck was entirely in God's hands. So, during the Golden Age of Piracy, leaving the ship for safety was an "every man for himself" situation.

In fact, the "women and children first" concept didn't emerge until 1852, when the British troopship Birkenhead sank off the coast of South Africa, and didn't have enough lifeboats for all of the British military personnel and their families on board.

Maritime law does not – and never has – required the captain to go down with his ship. However, he is supposed to be certain that all passengers are evacuated from the ship, before he abandons it.

Abase

To lower the flag on a ship.

Abate

To beat down, or to destroy, usually talking about a fortification or castle. When a storm abates, it's diminished.

Abel Brown

> Any pirate trying to achieve a very close personal
> acquaintance, usually brief, with a maiden.
> Usually, "He's pulling an Abel Brown," or "That
> one's an Abel Brown." Refers to the sea song or
> shanty, Abel Brown. (See the section about pirate
> songs and shanties.)

Aboard

> On or in any vessel, usually a ship. Close aboard
> means near the ship.

Above board

> Out in the open, honest, or on deck where
> everyone can see.
>
> Two stories of the phrase's origins:
>
> 1. From sailing, referring to everyone being on the
> deck where they could be seen. No pirates were
> hiding below deck.
> 2. From card games, where both hands were
> above the table (or board) so no cheating was
> going on.
>
> Opposite: Under board, below board, beneath the
> board, under hand, under the table.

Absentee pennant

> Pennant or flag flown to indicate that the captain
> or commanding officer is not on board. Or, any
> signal that the alpha male isn't near enough to be
> a problem.

Accommodations

> Ship's cabins outfitted for the comfort of passengers.

Accompany

> To sail together, as a company (or convoy) of ships.

Ack-men, Ack-pirates

> Thieves or pirates who ply their trade on fresh water, such as rivers. From the 16th-century term "acker," meaning tidal rivers.

Acrostolium

> Before ships had figureheads, the prow of the ship displayed a symbol of war or power – like a shield or a helmet -- called an acrostolium.

Act of Grace, Act of Pardon

> A document declaring a privateer absolved of any crimes at sea, also described as "a general pardon and act of oblivion." The Act was formally part of the English constitution written in 1653, as an Institution of Government. Sometimes referred to as an Act of Pardon, the 1652 and 1660 law formally called "An Act of Free and General Pardon, Indemnity, and Oblivion." An Act of Grace could also pardon deserters. Also see Letter of Marque.

Action

> A battle or fight. Someone in "active service" was engaged in (or preparing for) a battle against the enemy.

Adamant

> First used to mean a white sapphire or diamond, and later – around the 14th century – used to mean a lodestone (also loadstone) or magnet (iron). A lodestone on a piece of wood, floating in water, was one of the earliest compasses and it was first used by Chinese sailors as early as the 6th century BCE.

> The attractive power of the magnet is called its alliciency.

Addle, Addel

> Liquid filth, usually referring to water that had gone putrid in the casks aboard ship, originally from a Swedish term for cow urine. (You're welcome for that visual, next time you look at beer.) Later, "addled" meant confused, such as when the brain had been corrupted by drink.

Addlings

> Accumulated pay, earnings, or wages held intact.

Admiralty

> The office in the British government responsible for overseeing the Royal Navy.

Adrift

> Loosened from moorings, floating without any attachment to the sea bed, dock, or another secure object. If someone hasn't a clue what he or she is doing, that person might be adrift.

Advance note

> When a sailor (or pirate crew member) signed on with a ship that issued articles or contracts, that note guaranteed the new crew member a month's wages, no matter what else happened.

> When danger was likely, the amount advanced might be two months' wages. Clearing those sums off the books was called working a dead horse, not to be confused with a similar expression about goats.

Afraid

> Among pirates, it's one of the worst possible insults, meaning cowardice.

Aft

> Towards the back of the ship or other vessel. Also see Abaft.

After-

> Used to indicate any part of the back part of the ship, such as the after-cabin, after-hatchway, after-guard, after-ladder, and so on.

Afternoon watch

Since at least 1450 and maybe earlier, a "watch" has meant to guard, or to remain awake and alert. The afternoon watch was usually between the hours of 1200 and 1600.

Aground

Since around 1500, this word has meant to rest on the strand (the land bordering a body of water, or the shore between the high and low tide lines), or in shallow water. (Also the origin of the term, "stranded.") Can also be used figuratively, to indicate a ship or boat that has been disabled.

When a ship has been stranded and the tide has gone out, she's "high and dry," or – using the term literally and figuratively – has little hope of quick recovery.

Ahoy

Since 1751 and perhaps earlier, this has been a nautical term and a call (or shout) used to draw attention, or to call someone aloft.

It has two roots in one word, "hoy." In the 14oos, it described a small, seagoing sloop or boat, used to transport people and goods.

In the 1600s, it was a shout to call attention or to drive hogs. (May be an early version of "Hi.")

"Ahoy" was Alexander Graham Bell's standard greeting when answering a telephone. Thomas Edison preferred "Hello," and that's the one that was popularized.

A hoyden means someone who is ill-bred, often a young woman who calls attention to herself.

Aiguades

A French port where a ship could restore its supply of water or other beverages. Sometimes slang for a port where liquor was plentiful and cheap.

Air-braving

Setting sail despite fierce or unfavorable winds. Figuratively, someone with courage in the face of the unknown.

Air funnel

Removing timber or planks from the deck of the ship, to allow fresh air into the hold. Today, certain bodily eruptions can cause automobile passengers to roll down the windows, creating a similar air funnel.

Airt, Art

Direction of the compass, such as north, south, east, or west.

A-lee, Lee, Leeward

On the sheltered side, away from the wind. Figuratively, it means cautious.

All at sea, or just "at sea"

> Adrift, confused.

All hands

> Everyone aboard, officers and crew, and
> sometimes passengers as well.

Allan

> Point or piece of land nearly surrounded by water,
> usually a tidal stream.

Allay

> To put to one side.

Aloft

> On the higher part of the ship, well above the
> deck. Since the late 16th century, it's meant
> anything that's up in the air, like a star.

Alonde

> On land, or ashore.

Alongshore

> Sailing in sight of the shoreline, and parallel to it.
> Along the shore.

Alongside

Side by side, usually referring to pulling up next to a ship or a pier.

Allowance

The portion of the provisions given to each member of the crew. Depending on his or her behavior, effort and contribution, that allowance might be double, full, two-thirds, half, or short.

Alphabetical list

A list of the entire crew, and everyone who was due to be paid (or given a share of the loot), and given a portion of the provisions.

Amalphitan Code, Amalfitan Code

Oldest known code of the sea, a set of sea laws compiled in the 11th century by the people of Amalphi (Amalfi), and observed by most Mediterranean countries.

Ambuscade

A group of men hiding in wait, to surprise the enemy and cut him off from his supplies, or rob him. Also, the location where the attackers hide. (Similar to ambush.)

Amidships, Midships

To or at the middle of the ship. (Not exactly the same as amidward, meaning towards or near the middle of anything, including a ship.)

Anan?

> Asked when an order wasn't understood. It's like
> asking, "What do you mean?" May derive from
> "Again...?"

Anchor

> Any instrument or appliance, usually a long shank
> with a hook-shaped end, that fixes a ship in one
> location by tethering it to the seabed or something
> solid attached to the earth.

Anchorage

> A place with adequate support to place an anchor
> that will fix a ship from drifting.

In the 19th century, the word was defined:

> "Ground which is suitable, and neither too deep,
> shallow, or exposed for ships to ride in safety
> upon; also the set of anchors belonging to a ship;
> also a royal duty levied from vessels coming to a
> port or road stead for the use of its advantages. It
> is generally marked on the charts by an anchor,
> and described according to its attributes of good,
> snug, open, or exposed."

Anchor's aweigh, away, a-weigh, a-trip, a-peak (a-pic)

> The anchor has cleared the ground, so the ship or
> vessel can drift or move freely. (There's some
> dispute over whether it's "anchor's away" or
> "anchor's aweigh.")

Anelace, Anclace

> The early name for a two-edged knife, dirk or dagger usually worn at the girdle. It's a term used rarely after the 15th century, repopularized by poets, especially in the 19th century.

Ankecher

> Handkerchief.

Anker

> A keg or cask holding about ten gallons, or 8 ½ imperial gallons. Used most often for brandy or wine.

Anniversary winds

> Winds, such as a monsoon, that blow predictably at a certain time of year. Anniversary winds were often the reason why pirate ships lingered around Madagascar – with its bars and gambling dens – after a successful engagement with East India Company vessels. (Well, that's their story and they're sticking to it.)

Answers her helm

> When a ship correctly responds to her rudder or steers. (In practical terms, she either answers or she doesn't. There are no voicemail or text options.)

A'n't

> Short version of "are not." Similar to "ain't," but
> without the harsh "ai" sound. (Sounds like "ant,"
> the insect.)

Anti-guggler

> A straw, siphon or narrow tube used to suck
> spirits from a bottle or other storage, usually as a
> way of taking more than the allowed provisions.
> It was designed to prevent the gurgling sound of
> liquid being removed and air entering the
> container.

Any port in a storm

> Making the best of the situation, finding a haven
> wherever one can.

Armaments

> A ship's weapons.

Arm chest

> A portable locker on the upper deck or tops for
> holding arms, and affording a ready supply of
> cutlasses, pistols, muskets or other weapons.

Arr, Harr, Yarr (and other variations)

> Yeah, yes, or a muttered acquiescence. In a
> movie, first said by Lionel Barrymore in the 1934
> movie, *Treasure Island,* in which Barrymore
> played the mysterious pirate, Billy Bones. (No one
> said "Arr!" in Stevenson's original book.)

This is different from "Arrgghh!" The latter is usually an expression of frustration. (Charlie Brown's Lucy says it often.)

As deaf as the main mast

Someone who consistently fails to understand or follow orders. (In case you hadn't noticed, pirates aren't very politically correct. Old pirate tales are full of expressions like this one.)

Ashore

On the beach, shore or land.

Astern

Toward the stern. A ship, an object or a vessel that is abaft (behind the mid-point of) another vessel or object.

Aswim

Afloat.

Athwart, Athwartships

At right angles to the fore and aft, or centerline, of a ship

Auk, or Awk

A sea bird with short wings, possibly Alca impennis and possibly extinct.

Avast

> Hold, stop, cease or desist from whatever is being done. Used at least since the late 17th century, possibly derived from "hold fast," or the Italian, "basta" (enough).

Away aloft

> The order to the men assigned to the rigging, to start up.

Away she goes

> When a ship, having stowed her anchor, fills and makes sail.

Aye

> Said once, it means "yes."

Aye, aye, or Aye, aye, sir

> Reply to an order or command. The first "aye" indicates that it was heard. The second "aye" means the order is understood and will be carried out. "Sir" is added when replying to an officer.

Ayond, Ayont

> Beyond, or at least on the far side of something.

B

Back and fill

> To take advantage of the tide being with you when the wind is not in your favor. To get windward in very narrow channels.

Back o' beyond

> A place that is a great distance away, and usually an unknown distance.

Bad berth

> A poor or rocky anchorage.

Baffling

> When the wind shifts from one point to another.

Baguio

> A rare but dreadfully violent wind among the Philippine Isles.

Bail'd, Bailed

> Expression, "I'll be bail'd," meaning "I'm honor-bound," or telling the truth.

Baitland

> A welcoming port where liquor flows freely.
> (Why... what kind of "bait" were you thinking of?)

Bale goods

> Merchandise packaged by the bale, bundle, or in packages, not in casks or cases.

To ballarag

> To bully or persecute.

Ballast

> Heavy weight stored in the lower part of the ship, keeping the ship upright. It's a counterbalance to the pull of the masts and the force of the wind in the sails, especially in high winds.

Bar

> Large mass of sand or earth, formed by the surge of the sea.

Barbary Coast, Berber Coast

> The coastal home of pirates and corsairs from the 16th century until around 1830 when the French invaded for the purpose of abolishing piracy. The Barbary Coast was composed of the seaboards of Algiers, Tunisia, and Tripoli (or Tripoly).

Bare-poles

> When a ship is at sea with no sails raised. (No comment about dancing options.)

Barking irons

> Large dueling pistols. Really large.

Barmy

> Slang for someone who's acting ridiculous or mad. Literally, someone who's full of barm. (Barm is the froth or head on any malt liquor beverage.) The expression originated in the 16th century.

Batten down the hatches

> Figuratively, get ready for trouble. Literally, when bad weather approached, the ship's hatches – where air entered from above deck to below – were covered with tarps and the tarps were secured with strips of wood (about one to three inches wide) called "battens."

Be

> In pirate talk, replaces most forms of the verb "to be," including is, are, was, were, will be, and so on.

Beaching a vessel

> Deliberately stranding a vessel or ship. Sometimes as a means of attack, sometimes done to your own ship to protect it from greater danger. Like a collision with the TARDIS.

Beacon

> Navigational light or marker.

Beakhead

> A protruding part of the front of the ship, usually directly above the figurehead. Sailors drilled holes in a board and mounted it at the beakhead so waste matter fell directly into the ocean. Hence, "the head" for the toilet.

Bear

> One of several expressions for a large, squared-off stone used for scraping clean the deck.

Bear down

> Turn away from the wind, often with reference to a transit.

Bearing

> The horizontal direction of a line of sight between two objects on the surface of the earth. In other words, which way it is or which way it's traveling.

Beaten back

> When a ship is forced to return to port due to bad weather. It's as good an excuse as any, when you realize your casks aren't as full or plentiful as they might be, for the trip ahead.

Beauty

> A woman, or anything that is stunningly impressive, and perhaps coveted. It's among the highest compliments.

Be-dundered

The condition of confusion or feeling stupefied, resulting from noise, often cannon fire. A "dunderhead" is someone often confused.

Belaying pins

Bars of iron or hard wood to which running rigging may be secured, or belayed.

Bent on a splice

Preparing for marriage. (A splice is used to join to ropes together.)

Bermuda squall

A sudden, strong wind experienced near the Bermudas. It's usually is preceded by heavy clouds, thunder, and lightning. It's a feature of the Gulf Stream, and it's sometimes felt as far as the banks of Newfoundland.

Berth

A bed on a boat, or a space in a port or harbor where a vessel can be tied up. The person who assigns sleeping berths is called the berther.

Between decks

The space between two whole decks. Also indicates someone whose role isn't clearly defined as part of the crew, someone who's neither here nor there.

Bilbo

> An old term for a flexible kind of cutlass, from
> Bilbao, where the best Spanish sword-blades were
> made. Shakespeare humorously describes Falstaff
> in the buck-basket, like a good bilbo. (I'm not
> sure if there's a literal hobbit connection. Tolkien
> was clever with words.)

Bilge

> The bottom of the ship's hull, or the lowest
> internal part of the hull. Figuratively, anything
> ridiculous, nonsense, or of no value, as in, "That's
> a lot of bilge." (Possibly referencing bilge water.)

Bilge fever

> When someone is ill from spending too much time
> in a foul hold. Exponentially worse than cabin
> fever.

Bilge rat

> A rat that lives in the bilge. More often, an insult
> suggesting that the person is the lowest of the
> low.

Bilge water

> The rain or seawater which occasionally enters a
> vessel, and running down to her floor, remains in
> the bilge of the ship until it is pumped out. It's
> usually dark, dirty-looking, and has a putrid odor.

Bindings

>The connecting parts of a ship or vessel, such as the beams, clamps, and transoms.

Binnacle

>The stand on which the ship's compass is mounted.

Binnacle list

>A ship's sick list, and men unfit for duty, kept at the binnacle.

Birlinn, Bior-linn

>16th century (or earlier) word for a large rowing boat using four to eight long oars rather than a sail, and usually from western Scotland or the Hebrides and manned by chieftains.

Bitts

>Posts mounted on the ship's bow. Usually two wooden uprights supporting a crossbar, for fastening ropes or cables.

Bitter end

>The anchor cable is tied to the bitts, when the cable is fully paid out, the bitter end has been reached. The last part of a rope or cable. Usually more trustworthy, since that part of the rope is rarely used.

Black's the white of my eye

> The same as saying, "I'm innocent."

Black spot

> A circular piece of cut paper or card, all black on one side and sometimes with a message on the other side. It means guilty, condemned, or – in the case of a captain – deposed.

> May have been invented by Robert Louis Stevenson for his book, Treasure Island. May be based on the tradition of showing a traitor, liar, or informer an Ace of Spades to signify that he's condemned. (Related to being "on the spot," or the single pip on that playing card.)

> Being "black spotted" meant the pirate was marked for death, by curse or by assassination.

> In Treasure Island, here's how the black spot was described:

> "It was around about the size of a crown piece. One side was blank, for it had been the last leaf; the other contained a verse or two of Revelation – these words among the rest, which struck sharply home upon my mind: 'Without are dogs and murderers.' The printed side had been blackened with wood ash, which already began to come off and soil my fingers; on the blank side had been written with the same material the one word 'Depposed.'" [Deposed.]

Blashy

> Watery, rainy (weather), flimsy, unreliable.

Blast!

> An expletive meaning hatred or extreme annoyance. (Also: Blast it! Blast it all! Blasted _____!)

Blethering, Blathering

> Talking aimlessly, speaking nonsense.

Blind harbour, Blind harbor

> A harbor with an entry concealed deliberately or by nature.

Blowe

> To chastise, scold or revile.

Blue Peter

> A blue flag with a white square in the center, hoisted when a ship is about to sail.

Blunt

> Money, especially coins.

Boanga

> A Malay pirate vessel, usually using oars rather than a sail, and keeping a very low profile until it's about to attack. Going Boanga means being very sneaky and clever.

Board him in the smoke

> To board an enemy ship by firing a broadside and using the cover of smoke to attack for hand-to-hand combat.

Boatswain, bosun, bos'n

> A non-commissioned officer responsible for the sails, ropes and boats on a ship who issues "piped" commands to seamen. Pronounced "BO-sunn."

Bole

> A small boat.

Bombo, Bumboo, Bimbo

> Weak, cold punch, sometimes worse than grog. Originally a mix of rum, water, sugar, and ground nutmeg, one of the earliest rum beverages.

> At best, it's roughly two parts rum to one part water. At worst, it's mostly water with a splash of dark rum and flavorings. Served cold.

> Recipe: 2 ounces of rum, one ounce of water, one teaspoon of sugar, and a dash of nutmeg.

(Variations: Use lemon juice instead of water, and grenadine instead of sugar, and dilute with water as necessary. Or, replace both the water and sugar with lemon-lime soda, to taste, and add cinnamon and nutmeg, also to taste.)

Bone

Good and ready. Or, a command. Also, a ship is said to "carry a bone in her mouth and cut a feather, when she makes the water foam before her." – William Dean Howells.

Booby

The tropical sea bird, Sula fusca. The name "booby" is derived from the way in which it allows itself to be caught immediately after settling. The direction in which the flies as evening comes on often shows where land may be found. (The "booby prize" is one of little value, earned with little or no effort.)

Booms

Spare masts or yards, kept in reserve on board the ship.

Booty

Treasure or plunder taken by thieves, or the spoils of war.

Boreas

> The god of the north wind, in the expression,
> ""Cold and chilly, like Boreas with an iceberg in
> each pocket." Sometimes the north wind itself.

Bouncer

> A gun with a very strong kick when fired.

Bow, Bough

> The shoulders or rounded front end of a ship.

Bow-chaser

> A small-bore gun or cannon placed at the bow of
> the ship to fire at an enemy ship ahead, damaging
> the other ship's sails or mast. Also called a chase,
> chaser, or chase-piece.

Bowse, Bouse

> To haul, pull or hoist, usually with a tackle.

Brake

> The handle or lever of the ship pump, by which it
> is worked.

Brass monkeys, Brass monkey weather

> Cold, raw, miserable weather. The "brass
> monkey" reference is disputed, but most agree
> that one source of the expression is a small
> cannon (or drake, or monkey), popularly called
> the brass monkey.

Breach of the sea, Breech of the sea

> Waves breaking over the hull of a vessel in bad weather, or when stranded.

Breaking liberty

> Not returning on schedule. Not quite mutiny, but it could be a first step.

Breath of wind

> Just slightly more breeze than dead calm.

Bridge

> A structure extending the full width of the vessel, above the weather deck. It houses a command center, itself called the bridge.

Bring to

> Cause a ship to be stationary. This can be achieved by a variety of means.

Bring up

> To stop. To cause a ship to be stationary by casting the anchor, or by running into rocks or shoals.

Broadside

> Fire all the artillery – guns and cannons -- on one side of a ship, all at once. (Exploding into space is optional.)

Brood hen star

> Cluster of the Pleiades, sometimes used for night navigation.

Brush

> A skirmish.

Buccaneer

> A pirate, originally those who roved and plundered the Spanish Main in the 17th century. The word came from *boucaniers,* a term given to French hunters who settled in or near St. Domingo and survived by farming, and by hunting wild cattle and then smoking the meat on racks. When the Spanish attacked and drove out these settlers, the displaced community took to the seas as buccaneers. Distinguished by their leather clothing. (The word *boucan* is related to *barbecue.* Buccaneers usually smoked their meat over a fire or hot coals.)

Bulk of the ship

> Entire cargo when it's stored in the hold.

Bulkhead

> An upright wall within the hull of a ship.

Bulwark

> The extension of the ship's side above the level of the weather deck.

Bumboat

A private boat selling small items, vegetables, and other provisions, to ships.

Bundle up

A call to the men to get up on deck, quickly.

Bung hole

A bung is a stopper or cork. The hole it goes into, usually in a cask or barrel, is the bung hole.

Buoy

A floating, navigational marker, usually anchored to the sea bed or other earthen object.

By the board

Anything that has gone overboard. (This is another expression with conflicting meanings, depending on the group using it. For some, "by the board" means something done according to the rules. For others, it's the opposite.)

C

Cabin

> An enclosed room on a deck or flat.

Cape Horn fever

> A false illness claimed by someone who only wants
> to avoid work.

Cap'n's daughter, Captain's daughter

> The naval cat, or a light cat o' nine tails, used for
> punishment.
>
> Might also refer to the punishment of being
> strapped to a gun (cannon) before being flogged
> with a cat o' nine tails. Some say that the
> "captain's daughter" was the largest gun aboard,
> exposing less of the back than the mast or a
> smaller cannon might.
>
> In more current slang, "kissing the cap'n's
> daughter," and variations, mean being punished.

Captain

> A leader of others, usually a military leader. The
> person in charge of a ship's crew.

Careen

> Turn the boat or ship on its side or upside down to
> scrape it clean of seaweed and barnacles, and
> make repairs. Barnacles or seaweed on the ship's
> hull will slow it, and pirate ships rely on speed.

Cat o' nine tails

> A disciplinary whip made by separating nine strands of a rope, and attaching them to a handle.
>
> In some cases, the sentence included being forced to craft the whip that would be used in the punishment.
>
> Some references go out of their way to stress that this was a cotton rope. (I can't imagine being disciplined with a limp cotton clothesline.) Other references show photos of what looks like a cat o' nine tails made from sisal rope.

Chain shot

> Usually two cannon balls linked with chain, and fired together at an enemy vessel. This was used to damage rigging and masts.

Chase guns

> Cannons mounted on the bow or stern. At the bow, the cannons could fire upon a ship ahead. Cannons at the rear could deter pursuing vessels.

Clean bill of health

> A certificate declaring that the ship, its crew and its passengers carry no infectious diseases. Issued by the port officer, usually before allowing anyone or anything off the ship.

Clean slate

At the helm, a slate was kept by the watch. On it, they recorded the details of the ship's speed, distance covered, headings, and so on. At the beginning of a new watch the slate was wiped clean, starting all over again.

Close quarters, close-fights

Since the mid-18th century, this has meant: when a ship drew close enough to its enemy to be able to engage in hand-to-hand combat. Direct contact with the enemy.

Club Hauling

The ship drops one of its anchors at high speed to turn abruptly. This was sometimes used as a means to quickly get a good firing angle on a pursuing vessel, and increase chances of victory.

Copper bottomed

Anything reliable, especially a ship sheathed on the bottom and sides with copper. That prevented an infestation of barnacles, and other deterioration from natural undersea creatures.

Oddly, a "copper captain" was defined as a sham, a cheat, or someone claiming the title under false pretenses.

Courses

> Points of the compass (17th century). Each of the sails attached to the lower yards of a ship; in the 16th century, this was the mainsail and foresail. Some also include the mizzen.

Coxswain, Cockswain

> The helmsman or crew member in command of a boat. (Said "COKK-sunn.")

Crimp

> A swindler or a cheat.

Crow's nest

> The highest lookout point on a mast, usually enclosed with a box or barrel for someone to stand in. Also a fort placed on a high location for best visibility.

Cur

> A mongrel dog or an unworthy person.

Cut and run, cut off, cut away

> To flee. Literally, to cut the rope, chain or cable attachment to the anchor, leaving it behind, and possibly causing damage to the rigging. It was the only way to make sail quickly, without waiting to haul up the anchor.

Cut of his jib

> Figuratively, one's appearance or how others judge the person. The jib is a distinctive sail, usually triangular, and could indicate both the nationality of a ship and, perhaps by prejudice, how well it was handled.

D - E

Davy Jones' Locker

> The bottom of the ocean, the grave of those who perish at sea.

> "The bottom of the sea, where nothing is lost, because you know where it is." – W. H. Smyth in The Sailor's Word-Book (1867).

> "Davy Jones" was supposed to be the spirit of the sea, or the devil who ruled the waters. The term may come from the concept of the Biblical Jonah, later called the Devil Jonah. (In the 1630s, Davy Jones was the name of a pirate, but he wasn't well-enough known to be credited with this reference.)

> Legends may have come from earlier, Celtic stories of the Ochren, which included underwater prisons made from bones.

Dead men

> Empty bottles, or sometimes empty casks, because (a pun) the "spirit" has left.

Deadlights

> Eyes. (Enunciate clearly. In slang, they're not the same thing as headlights.)

Decks

> The horizontal surfaces in the ship's general
> structure. Unlike flats, they are a structural part of
> the ship.

Deep six

> To throw something (or someone) overboard. A
> fathom is about six feet deep, so a "deep six" is
> something more than six feet – a fathom – deep.
> In some slang, it means to get rid of someone or
> something, by any means necessary and
> expedient.

Derelict

> Anything abandoned at sea.

> Also refers to the 1901 musical, Treasure Island,
> that popularized a song, Derelict, with the lyrics,
> "Fifteen men on a dead man's chest, yo-ho-ho and
> a bottle of rum."

Dogwatch

> A short, two-hour watch. Used to adjust the
> watch schedule for meals, or other times when the
> usual four-hour watch was a problem.

Doubloons

> A Spanish gold coin equal to 128 reales, or 16
> pieces of eight.

Draft

The depth of a ship's keel below the waterline.

Dressing down

Beating or criticizing. Or, treating the surface of old sails to renew them. In some cases, renewing or at least working on the surface of other things, as well.

Driver

A boat used for fishing with a net. Synonym for a spanker, a sail used at the rear of the ship, especially the large sail flown from the mizzen gaff.

Even keel

When the keel of the ship is parallel to the horizon. Smooth sailing.

F

False colors

> The pirate practice of flying whatever flag seemed most likely to allow the pirate ship to draw close to its intended target. At the last minute, the pirates would replace the false flag with their captain's flag or their ship's flag, such as a Jolly Roger.

Fathom, fathom out

> To get a sense of or to measure, figuratively or literally. Originally, the average distance between a man's outstretched hands – approximately six feet – or, in earlier times, what could be enclosed within a man's arms.

> Men would embrace one another, each to "fathom" or estimate the strength of his companion.

Fiddler's Green

> The personal heaven of pirates, with plenty of wine, women and song.

Figurehead

> Symbolic image at the head of a traditional sailing ship.

Fireship

> A ship loaded with flammable materials and explosives and set to drift into an enemy port or fleet. It was set alight at the last minute, with any crew escaping to safety before it explodes. Also, slang for venereal disease.

First rate

> The classification for the largest sailing war vessels of the 17th through 19th centuries.

First Mate

> The second in command of a ship, after the captain. John Paul Jones was a first mate at age 19, and was in command of the West Indian trade ship, the "John," at age 21.

Flag hoist

> Signal flags strung together to convey a message.

Flash in the pan

> Anything of short duration, especially something that started with great promise. When gunpowder in a flintlock's priming pan is ignited, but it doesn't set off the charge.

Fluke

> The wedge-shaped or pointed part of an anchor's arms. The part of the anchor that digs into the seabed or otherwise gets hooked around something secure.

Fly by night

>A large sail employed for sailing downwind. It usually required little attention, so even the drowsiest or most irresponsible night watch could be trusted with it.

Fore

>Short for "forward" or towards the front (bow) of the boat. Also, as "a'fore," it means "before."

Fouled

>Spoiled, jammed, tangled, ruined, or otherwise made unusable.

French leave

>When a sailor leaves his post (or, usually, the ship) – with or without permission – intending to return, preferably without his absence being noticed.

Furner

>One who cooks bread in his own oven. Extended to mean a ship purchased (not stolen) by its captain.

Foot

>The bottom of a ship's sail.

Footloose

> When the foot (or bottom) of a ship's sail is not secured properly, it is footloose, blowing around in the wind.

Forecastle

> A short, raised deck, above the upper deck and at the head of the vessel. Originally used to command the enemy's decks. Later, this was the forward part of the ship, under the deck, where most of the sailors were berthed. (Say the word, slurred. Enunciating it clearly is a sure sign of a landlubber.)

Fore

> Towards the bow (of the vessel).

G

Gaff

> The spar used to extend the ship's sails. Also a barbed, long hook with a sharp point to haul fish in.

Galleot

> Smaller, single-deck version of a galley-style ship, and favored by Mediterranean pirates due to its faster speed and lower maintenance.

Galley

> A ship, including large, early warships with one or more banks of oars. Also a large, open row boat for river navigation, or even a large pleasure boat.
>
> Later, the word was commonly used to mean the kitchen or hearth where food is cooked on the ship.
>
> Note: A galley slave was one sentenced to row a galley ship, not someone assigned KP duty.
>
> A galley man was someone who rowed in a galley ship, voluntarily and for pay or for part of the loot. However, the phrase "galley man" also meant any trader, especially a corsair, who arrived in port with plunder to sell or trade.

Gangway!

> Clear a path.

Garbled, Garboiled

The illegal practice of mixing cargo with garbage. In piracy, this practice could make a cargo seem larger or better than it was. In sailing, it's also a last-ditch (and rare, really impractical) way to keep unsecured items in the hold from sliding into each other, by storing garbage between them. Figuratively, the term means something that's confusing.

Gentleman o' fortune

Euphemism meaning a pirate.

Get underway

To begin moving through the water (also "get under sail"), or figuratively, to start something. Some spell it "underweigh" or "under weigh."

Go on the account, Going on account

Initially, joining a pirate crew. In later use, when someone quit the Royal Navy and took to the high seas as a pirate. In addition, I found references to it being a phrase a captain used when planning a risky expedition, and looking for volunteers. Only those who took part in that raid or expedition would claim the greater portion of the loot from it.

"They were rigorously governed by an iron hand and by the unwritten 'code of honor'. A pirate entered upon 'the account' (a term meaning piracy) by taking the oath of fealty to the cause, abjuring all social ties, pledging himself never to desert his ship or defraud his comrades or steal anything belonging to his fellows. – from Pirates and Piracy, by Oscar Herrmann (1902)

Grapeshot

Small balls of lead fired from a cannon to hurt people, rather than cause structural damage. The balls of lead tend to spray, similar to shot from a shotgun, but on a larger scale.

Grog

Weak spirits, usually rum diluted with water.

Recipe: Mix 2 ounces of dark rum and 1/2 ounce of fresh lime juice. Dissolve 1 teaspoon dark brown sugar in 4 ounces hot water, and add to the rum-lime mixture. Garnish with a slice of orange and a cinnamon stick. Add more brown sugar, rum, or lime juice, to taste.

From the infamous Captain's Order Number 349 (21 August 1740), by Admiral Edward Vernon:

"You are hereby required and directed ... that the respective daily allowance ... be every day mixed with the proportion of a quart of water to a half pint of rum, to be mixed in a scuttled butt kept for that purpose, and to be done upon the deck, and in the presence of the Lieutenant of the Watch who is to take particular care to see that the men are not defrauded in having their full allowance of rum... and let those that are good husbanders receive extra lime juice and sugar that it be made more palatable to them."

Watered-down Pusser's rum - half a gill with equal part of water issued to all seamen over twenty.

Groggy

Drunk or addle-headed from having consumed a lot of grog.

Gunwale

Upper edge of the hull. (Usually pronounced, "gunnell.")

H - I

Half-cocked

> Keeping your flintlock partially cocked so it's ready to fire on short notice. Figuratively, someone who's wound up; an outburst is imminent.

Halyard, Halliard, Haulyard

> A rope-and-tackle used to raise or lower a sail, sometimes with the spar already attached.

Hand

> A member of the crew.

Haul wind

> A command to point the ship so as to be heading in the same direction as the wind, to maximize speed.

Hawse-hole

> Holes in a ship's bow, each cut for a cable to pass through. Generally to raise and lower the anchor.

Hazard, Hazzard

> Since the 16th century, a game of chance involving two dice and rules that vary widely, often changed on the fly. Likewise, to put something at risk, as in a game of chance.

Head

> The toilet or latrine of a vessel, sometimes short for beakhead (see definition, above).

Headsail

> Any sail, usually of a smaller size, flown in front of the most forward mast.

Hearties

> A brave man of the sea. Those with heart and those who remain loyal.

Heave ahead

> To pull the boat or ship forward by pulling on the rope or chain attached to the anchor. (The anchor will be somewhere astern the ship, usually a short distance ahead.)
>
> (Heave astern = backwards; Heave to = stop.)

Hold

> In earlier use, below the orlop deck, the lower part of the interior of a ship's hull. Often, it was used exclusively for cargo. Later, especially in merchant vessels (as opposed to warships) it extended up through the decks to the underside of the weather deck.

Holystone

> A chunk of sandstone, about the size of a Bible, used to scrub the decks in a kneeling, prayerful position. (Also referred to as a bear, or a bearstone.)

Hornpipe

> A sailor's dance, usually like a jig. There are many variations, but here's one of the simplest: First you touch the deck with your right heel, then hop straight up in the air and land with your right toe touching the deck. Then, you hop to put the weight on your right leg repeat the motion with your left foot – heel, toe – and go back to your right.

> (Then again, it might be toe, heel... blame it on dyslexia. Or the grog. Or both.)

> The pace is fairly quick and it should always be learned with a dancing instructor. Land on your foot the wrong way, and it's easy to break something. (Not that Grace O'Blarney has ever done that. Ahem.)

> Also a "hornpipe" is the name of the musical instrument played during the dance. It's a single-reed instrument, sounding more like a whistle or a tiny bagpipe than a flute.

Hornswoggler, Hornswaggler

> A 19th-century term meaning anyone who cheats, lies, or swindles others.

Hull

> The body, shell and basic framework of the ship, excluding the masts, the sails, and rigging.

In the offing

> In the water visible from a ship. The offing is the water away from the shore, and usually beyond the general anchoring ground. Figuratively, something that's about to happen.

J - K

Jack

A small flag, usually smaller than the ensign. On a ship, usually a small flag identifying nationality. Flown from the jack-staff at the bow of the ship.

This word could also be used to describe a sailor. The flag was considered a member of the crew, so this definition fits both.

Jack Tar or Jack Afloat are also words meaning a sailor. Jack Ketch is usually the hangman, so you never want to "dance with Jack Ketch."

Jib

A triangular stay-sail at the very front of a ship. Also, to pull a sail from one side of a ship to the other, for the purpose of tacking.

Roger

a pirate's flag. "Roger" was slang for a sailor, v someone – possibly impressed -- in the avy.   So, the "jolly roger" might first t the grinning skull and crossbones on around, also the most popular of a jolly roger, today.

Keel

> The lowest timber of a ship, forming a central ridge, and the structural basis of the hull.

Keelhaul

> Punishment usually resulting in death by tying the condemned to a rope and dragging him along the barnacle-covered hull of the ship.

Kickshaw

> Something that barely matters. Also refers to French cooking.

Kill-devil

> New rum. Slang for anything ingested, especially liquor, that's dangerous, unhealthy, toxic or fatal.

Killock

> A small anchor. In modern use, a derogatory term for other things; seriously, one would never have a right grand killock.

Kraken

> A legendary sea monster, perhaps like an octopi initially reported near Norway and Greenland. officially designated *Microcosmus marinus.* In Icelandic lore, may be the same as the *hafgu* though that's also associated with underwat' trolls or Sea Trows.

Kraken may be based in sightings of giant squid, which can achieve a size of 50 feet.

Then again, some of us believe the Kraken is exactly what the pirates have always said it is: A monster from the deep.

Know the ropes

A sailor who "knows the ropes" is familiar with the ropes and knots that are part of everyday use aboard any ship. (However, this phrase may originate with theatre terms, where curtains and sets were managed with ropes, as well.)

L

Lady bird

> A prostitute, a woman of easy virtue, also called a "lightskirt." Some insist that the term was one of endearment, as used in Shakespeare's *Romeo and Juliet,* but that can be disputed.

Landlubber

> Anyone who doesn't meet the basic requirements of a pirate, usually someone who's new to the sea. (A "lubber" is someone clumsy who doesn't work and doesn't pull his own weight, no matter where he is.)

Lanyard, Laniard, Lanniers

> A rope or line, usually attached to something, and used as a handle or carrier.

Larboard

> When facing the front of the ship, it's usually the left side of the ship. Possibly started as the lading board, indicating the side of the ship where cargo was loaded.

Lass

> An unmarried woman, usually a girl.

Lay down

> To start something. To begin building a ship is to lay it down.

League

A unit of distance, usually three nautical miles or 3,041 fathoms. On land, about three miles.

"Seven league boots" usually describe someone of enormous size or ability to cover distance quickly. Translated from a French expression, *bottes de sept lieues.* In English use, originated in a 1799 fairy tale, Hop o My Thumb, where magical boots allowed the wearer to cover seven leagues – 21 miles – with each step.

Lee side

The side of the ship that's turned away from the wind. (Also see Leeward.) The other side, facing into the wind, is the weatherly side or the windward side.

Lee shore

The shore that's downwind of a ship. A ship which cannot sail well to windward risks being blown onto a lee shore. Once there, the ship is likely to run aground or become stranded.

Leeway

How much a ship is blown leeward by the wind. Figuratively, giving someone a little extra room for error.

Leeward

The direction that the wind is blowing towards, or the side of the ship that's sheltered from that wind. If the wind is blowing from the east (towards the west), the west side of the ship will be sheltered from the wind, so it's the leeward side.

Let go and haul

The ship is in line with the wind. It's time to let go and move quickly towards the destination.

Letter of Marque and Reprisal

A license granted to a privateer permitting him and his crew to attack enemy ships, claim their cargo, and bring that ship's crew back to stand trial. If there was a gateway to piracy, this was certainly it.

Sailing as a privateer under a Letter of Marque and Reprisal was considered honorable and patriotic work, in addition to being very profitable. This was formally sanctioned as early as the reign of Edward III (14th century). However, records show that licensed reprisal was authorized by Edward I (13th century) and perhaps earlier.

Reprisal is to seize the property and sometimes the people of an enemy country, as compensation for injuries caused by their countrymen.

Marque – from words indicating boundaries and including the right to seize those who cross them – later indicated that the ship (and its captain) had also been authorized to arm itself and set out to attack and capture enemy ships.

In France, a similar authorization was a *lettre de marque* or a *lettre de course.* The latter was the probably origin of the expression "corsairs," for Mediterranean pirates.

In 1856, these practices were formally abolished throughout European nations. (Informally... that might be another matter.)

Letting the cat out of the bag

Betraying a trust or giving out secrets. Punishment usually meant a flogging, signaled by taking the cat o' nine tails out of its storage bag.

Light along!

A request or order to give assistance, usually helping to lift something.

Lily-livered

Someone with no courage.

Line

A general term for any rope, cord, or string used aboard a ship. Specific lines will have names describing what they're made of, where they're used, and what their purpose is.

Linkister

> An interpreter, a linguist, or someone who knows the language and can translate for others.

List

> When a ship tilts or careens to one side.

> A roll of names, such a the list of crew members, or a list of those injured and excused from regular duties.

> Also, short for "enlist." Example: "If ye di'n't want to go t' sea, why'd ye list?"

Lloyd's

> Since 1601 – and some would argue, much earlier – the leading British insurer of goods, including those transported by ship. Started as a coffeeshop owned by Edward Lloyd.

Loaded to the Gunwales (said like, "Gunnels")

> An expression meaning extremely drunk. Literally, it's when the ship was so full, the cargo was loaded as high as the ship's rails.

Lob, Lob-cock

> Someone stupid and slow, similar to a lubber.

Loggerhead

> In whaling, after the whale was harpooned, the line would be attached to a heavy timber on board – called a loggerhead – that wouldn't move, no matter how much strain was put on it.

> Today, to be "at loggerheads" with someone means to argue with someone when the other party won't budge.

> Totally different from being a lager-head.

Loose cannon

> On ships, cannons were mounted on rollers and secured with a rope or cable to keep them under control during recoil. If the cannon broke free, it was able to roll around the deck and cause damage. Today, the expression also means someone or something unpredictable, risky, and in need of close supervision.

Lying on his oars

> Taking a break or getting some rest.

M

Maiden

> Any fortress or stronghold which has never been taken.

Main

> Usually a continent or the mainland, but it can also mean the ocean, especially when described in terms of the nearest mainland.

Mainmast

> The tallest mast on a ship.

Main-deck

> In a man-of-war ship, it's the deck immediately below the spar deck. In other ships, it's the part of the upper deck between the poop and the forecastle.

Main-yard men

> Crew members who are sick and unable to carry out their full orders.

Make free with the land

> Head towards shore.

Make water

> Describes when a ship is leaking.

Man-of-war

> An armed vessel equipped for attack. Also a term for any fighting man, or a sailor serving on a man-of-war. Any ship in the Royal Navy. (Plural: Men-of-war.)

> The deadly sea creature, the Portuguese man-of-war (or man o' war, or Bluebottle) is the Physalia physalis, looks like a jellyfish but it's actually composed of a group of zooids.

Make land

> To spot (or see) land from the ship, and usually to head towards it with the intention of dropping anchor.

Marches

> Border of a country, as the marches of Spain.

Marined

> Describes any animal that has a lower body like a fish, such as a mermaid.

Mariner

> An able, skilled and certified as a competent seaman, as opposed to someone who is simply a sailor.

Marish

> Describes marshy land, usually at the coast. May also refer to something salty.

Maroon

To abandon, usually on an island.

"The severest punishment to a member of the crew for thieving from a fellow-pirate was marooning — slitting the ears and nose and depositing the offender upon some desolate island or lonely shore with but few provisions and limited ammunition."   – from *Pirates and Piracy,* by Oscar Herrmann (1902)

According to Smyth (1867), "A custom among former pirates, of putting an offender on shore on some desolate cape or island, with a gun, a few shot, a flask of powder, and a bottle of water."

Sometimes, a pirate asked to be marooned. That's what happened when Alexander Selkirk was sailing with pirate William Dampier. Selkirk asked to be left on the uninhabited island of Juan Fernandez, Dampier was happy to do exactly that. (He and Selkirk argued a lot, so Dampier was glad to be rid of him.) Too late, Selkirk changed his mind, and it was four years until he was rescued. His story inspired Daniel Defoe's novel, *Robinson Crusoe.*

To marl

Drench a fish in vinegar so it can be eaten cold.

Mast

> A vertical timber or pole on a ship. It supports sails or rigging.

Matey

> Shipmate.

Me

> My or mine. Example: Me hearties, meaning my loyal friends. (Like the word "the" replaced by "th'," there are times when you'll replace "my" with just "m'," said like "muh.")

Merry dancers

> Northern lights (aurora borealis).

Mess

> Where the crew took their meals, usually near the galley.

Mew

> Seagull.

Mile

> A nautical mile is 6075.6 feet , instead of the land mile which is 5280 feet.

Minion

> A four-pounder gun, about seven feet long.

Mizzenmast

> On a three-masted ship, the mast at the rear.

Monger

> A trader. For example, a *fishmonger* trades in fish.

Mooney

> Not falling-down drunk yet, but unfit for duty, anyway.

Moonish

> Variable or moody.

To moor

> To secure a ship, usually with anchors or cables.

Motley crew

A mismatched crew, often dressed very differently. (A pirate's style of dress usually revealed where he was from.)

Mutchkin

> A one-pint measure.

Muzzle

> To drink too much.

Muzzy

Dull, stupid, gloomy, or half-drunk.

N - O

Nail

> As a measure of weight, it's about eight pounds.
> In past pirate days, the expression "to nail"
> someone was to hold him to a bargain or
> agreement.

Nake!

> An order to unsheathe swords and prepare to
> fight. (Refers to making the swords naked.)

Nancy

> A small lobster.

Nantz

> Brandy.

Naufragiated

> Shipwrecked. Today, being "a little naufragiated"
> means slightly the worse for drink.

Nautical day

> From noon to noon.

Navigant

> A sailor.

Navy

> Any assembly of ships, including merchant and military ships.

Neptune's sheep

> White foam on the crest of waves, also called white horses.

Nightcap

> Warm grog consumed immediately before going to bed.

Nitty

> A small, annoying noise or a squabble.

No quarter given

> When an enemy who surrenders is spared death, but that's the limit of the pirates' generosity. Resistance of any kind means immediate death.

No room to swing a cat

> When the crew was called to witness a flogging – usually required during punishment -- if the deck was too crowded for the bosun to swing the cat o' nine tails.

> Today, it's any cramped or confined area, where someone with claustrophobia might break out in a cold sweat.

Noggin

>A small measure of liquid, usually about ¼ cup.
>Also slang for someone's head or forehead.

Nogging

>Warming a beverage, usually alcohol, by the fire
>in the ship's galley.

No-howish

>When someone feels like he's coming down with
>an illness, but can't identify the symptoms yet.

O! or Ho!

>Said to get attention, usually indicating that the
>person should stop.

Oar, to shove in

>To give an opinion without being asked. Usually
>an unwelcomed opinion, as in, "Avast! 'Tis no time
>to be shovin' in yer oar."

Oars!

>Stop rowing and lift your oars out of the water.

Off

>Opposite of near. "Nothing off!" is an order to the
>helmsman not to let the ship drift out of the wind.

Old country

> References England or Great Britain, when in the Americas. Never used for any part of Europe or the rest of the world.

On either tack

> Any way or either way. To accomplish something any way you can.

Open lower deckers

> Fire the lower guns. Also slang for someone who uses violent language.

Orc, ork

> In the earliest use (1590), it meant a monster or ogre, especially those that weren't discriminating in their food choices. Later (1611), it meant a sea monster.

> The word was later used in the Latin as orca, meaning a whale.

> In later nautical use, orc could also mean seaweed, especially when enough was tangled on the hull to put the ship at risk.

> Did Tolkien deliberately use that word? Maybe.

Orisont

> Horizon. Probably an early spelling of the modern word.

Out-boats

> The order to hoist out the boats.

Overbear

> One ship overbears another if she can carry more sail in a fresh wind. Or, to sail downwind of another ship, stealing the wind from its sails.

Over-boyed

> When the captain and majority of the crew are very young.

Over-masted

> When a ship's mast is too high or too heavy, and causes balance problems for the ship.

Overreach

> When tacking, to hold a course too long.

Over the barrel

> When a crew member, usually a boy, was held over the barrel of a gun for beating or flogging.

Overwhelmed

> Capsized, foundered, or when a ship is overtaken by too many waves. Used in the song lyrics, "Lash'd to the helm, should seas o'erwhelm."

P - Q

Pace

A measurement of distance, somewhere between two-and-a-half and three feet.

Parley, Parlay, Parler, Parlez

A discussion or talk. From the French verb, parler, "to talk."

Among men of the sea, a parley was signaled by a drum beat, letting an enemy know that a conference was requested... or demanded.

Parole

Word of honor given by a prisoner, until he's returned to his own country or ship.

Part brass rags

End a friendship. Comes from the practice of assigning two men to cleaning duty. They'd share cleaning supplies, including rags for polishing brass. A friend who shared this duty with you was called a brassie. (In modern times, the expression for a falling-out, parted brass rags, was popularized by author P. G. Wodehouse.)

Patacoon

Another word for a Spanish piece of eight.

Pedro-a-pied, Pedro-pee

Proving you're sober enough for duty, by standing on one leg while walking a plank, or putting one foot precisely in front of the other while walking a single plank. Also called treading a seam.

Percer

A rapier or short sword.

Perry

A sudden squall.

Picarry

Piracy on a small scale, mostly thieving.

Pieces o' eight

A Spanish coin that was worth eight reales, and it could be cut into pieces (up to eight) as smaller denominations. Eight reales is equal to one dollar. Pieces of eight were accepted as currency, worldwide, between the 17th and 19th centuries. That made them ideal for pirates, so they could spend wherever they landed.

Today, the phrase is slang for coins or money in general.

Pilot

> Navigator, usually someone qualified and knowledgeable about the channels and waterways in the area where the ship is traveling. An experienced person charged with the ship's course near the coast.

Pinch-gut pay

> When the sailor's allowance (pay) was very small. The person dispensing that pay was called a pinch gut.

Pipe

> A whistle used by boatswains (bosuns or bos'ns) to issue commands. The commands varied in pitch and length.

Pipe down

> A signal on the bosun's pipe to signal the end of the day. All members of the crew – with the possible exception of the night watch -- should extinguish all lights and go silent.

Pirate

> "An armed ship that roams the seas without any legal commission, and seizes or plunders every vessel she meets; their colours are said to be a black field with a skull, a battle-axe, and an hour-glass." – W. H. Smyth in *The Sailor's Word-Book.*

Pitch

> The rocking movement of the ship from front to back, especially when the bow of the ship is plunged into the waves.

Poop, Poop deck

> The aftermost and highest part of a large ship's hull. Also, a deck raised over the after-part of a spar-deck, sometimes called the round-house.

Port

> When facing the front of the ship, the port side is the left-hand side of the ship facing forward. This was previously called the larboard.

Powder monkey

> The boy or sailor who supplies powder to the gunners. Today, slang for anyone procuring provisions like food or drink.

Press gang

> Wharf laborers whose job was to recruit sailors by any means – usually by force or by getting them drunk – and authorized by the Impress Service of the Royal Navy. The service was looking for "eligible men of seafaring habits, between ages 18 and 45," though that definition was sometimes stretched.

The practice of impressment was legally sanctioned as early as the 13th century in England, under Edward I, and was mostly discontinued after 1815.

Privateer

A sailor or ship captain with a contract (Letter of Marque) from a government, authorizing him or her to attack enemy ships, and share the plunder with the authorizing government.

Purser rigged and parish damned

Describes a man who went to sea to escape troubles – legal or marital – on land.

Press gang

Wharf laborers whose job was to recruit (press) sailors by any means – usually by force or by getting them drunk – and authorized by the Impress Service of the Royal Navy. The service was looking for "eligible men of seafaring habits, between ages 18 and 45," though that definition was sometimes stretched.

The practice was legally sanctioned as early as the 13th century in England under Edward I, and was mostly discontinued after 1815.

Privateer

A sailor or ship captain with a contract (Letter of Marque) from a government, authorizing him or her to attack enemy ships, and share the plunder with the authorizing government.

Also called a private man-of-war.

Prolly

Probably. Anything capable of being proved.
Example: "Ev'n if'n the cap'n's prolly wrong, he's
right."

Prow

Another word for the bow of the ship.

Purser rigged and parish damned

Describes a man who went to sea to escape
troubles – legal or marital – on land.

Quade

Unsteady.

Quarantine

Isolation for up to 40 days, to prevent the spread
of disease. Can include people, goods, and cargo.
Terms of quarantine date back to Venice in the
15th century, or perhaps earlier.

Quost

Coast. "Quost" is the old spelling.

R

Ransack

> To search for something stolen or missing, or to
> search for something worth stealing. To pillage.
>
> To ransack the hold is to reorganize it so the
> space is better utilized.

Rapparee

> A smuggler, or someone who uses his wiles or
> coercion to obtain hospitality. An irregular soldier
> or freebooter. (A freebooter is a word used since
> the late 17th century to describe a pirate.)

Rais, Reis

> A sea captain of the Muslim world. (Example: The
> brothers Barbarossa.) From the Arab word for
> head, the terms means the captain of a boat or
> vessel, or a chief or governing leader.

Razed

> Completely demolished.

Ready about!, or Ready oh!

> Every man to his station, preparing to tack.

Redhibition

> To set aside a contract of sale.

Rendezvous

> A location where a group of ships gather to form a company.

Rigged

> Completely equipped.

Rigging

> The system of masts and lines on ships and other sailing vessels.

Right up and down

> When the winds are at dead calm.

Roll

> A vessel's motion tilting from side to side. If you were on deck and facing the front of the ship, the roll would cause you to lean to the right, then to the left, and back again.

Rooming

> When the ship is running to leeward. (See leeway.)

Ropes

> Cordage above one inch in circumference, used to rig a ship.

In some contexts, cordage is a "rope" when it's stored. When it's put into use, it's called by its proper name, such as sheet, line, rigging, etc.

Rough knots, Rough nauts

Inexperienced seamen.

Round dozen

A punishment of 13 lashes.

Round house

Square cabins built on the after-part of the quarter-deck, and having the poop for its roof.

Round robbin

A way of signing a complaint in a circular manner so no one can tell who signed it first. From the French, ruban rond, or "round ribbon."

Roundly

Quickly.

Row dry!

An order to rowers, not to splash water into the boat.

Ruffle

A low, continuous vibrating sound of a drum, like a drum roll but quieter, that compliments the captain or ship's officers.

Rumbo

>   Rope stolen from a royal dockyard or storehouse.

Rummage sale

>   The sale of damaged cargo at distressed prices.
>   The expression comes from the French arrimage,
>   which meant to stow something. (To rummage
>   was to search for stolen goods.)

Run a rig

>   To run a scam, play a trick, or deliberately fool
>   someone.

S

Saber, Sabre

> A sword with a broad and rather heavy blade, thick at the back and curved towards the point, intended for cutting more than for thrusting.

Safe conduct

> A pass given to someone assuring him or her safe passage through enemy territory.

Sail ho!

> Alert given when a ship is spotted, but it's too far away to identify.

Sail-maker

> Skilled crew member assigned – with others – to maintain, repair, and mend the sails, and make new ones as necessary. The person in charge was often given the nickname, "Sails."

Sail-plan

> Drawings or plans showing which sail combinations to use in which situations.

Sails (commands)

> To "loose sail" is to let the sails hang in the wind, to dry or to prepare to make sail.
>
> To "make sail" is to spread the sails to begin sailing or increase speed.

To "shorten sail" is to take in some or all of the sails, to slow the ship or bring it to a standing stop.

To "strike sail" is to lower the uppermost sails, often as a salute to a nearby ship.

Sails (some names)

Four lower sails: Jib, jumbo foresail, mainsail. Four light sails: Balloon, fore gaff topsail, fisherman's flying staysail, main gaff topsail.

Sangaree

In its earliest form, it seems to have been an alcoholic mixed drink using arrack (not the Middle Eastern kind), citrus fruits, spices, cane sugar and water.

By the 18th century, it was described as a beverage from the Indies, composed of port or madeira (or Batavia Arrack, the forerunner of rum), water, lime-juice, sugar, and nutmeg, with an occasional corrective of spirits. The name comes from sangre, meaning red, the color of the drink.

Recipe: Mix together 1 ½ to 2 ounces dark rum, 1 ounce madeira, and ½ ounce fresh lime juice. Stir in 1 teaspoon of sugar, plus freshly grated nutmeg to taste. Finish by adding 2 or more ounces of chilled, still water, to taste.

Purists will quickly remind you that this is *not* the same thing as modern-day sangria.

Saraband, Sarabande

> A dance performed at the forecastle, very loosely based on a North African dance. Formally performed in triple metre, sometimes with castanets, including slow glides and fast changes from toe-out to toe-in positions. In 1583, Spain banned the dance for obscenity.

Savvy

> To understand. (As a question, it's usually just, "Savvy...?") From the French word, savoir, to know, to taste (often, figuratively), or to understand.

Scallywag, Scallawag, Scalliwag

> A scoundrel, disreputable fellow or mischief-maker.

To scour the seas

> To live the pirate's life, on the ocean.

Scud

> Low clouds in a squall.

Scuppers

> An opening on the side rail that allows water to run off the deck.

Scuttlebutt

> Gossip, tales, or rumors. Water was stored in a butt (a cask) and it was scuttled (a hole bored in it) so people could get drinking water. So, this was the pirate version of conversation around the water cooler.

Shakes
> Cracks or rents in any piece of timber. Extensive damage could make the timber worthless; some say that is the origin of the phrase, "No great shakes." More likely, that expression comes from games of dice, where the thrower consistently shakes a low score.

Sea

> After the ocean, the next largest body of water.

Sea gate, Sea gait

> When two boats are thrown together as a result of a long, rolling swell in the ocean.

Settling

> Sinking in the water.

Seven Seas

> This is an expression that can mean the known, vast bodies of water. Depending on the culture and context, it can be something literal or symbolic, too. Currently, there are at least five different lists of "the seven seas."

In Medieval times, the Arabian seven seas were:

1. Adriatic Sea.
2. Arabian Sea (Indian Ocean).
3. Black Sea.
4. Caspian Sea.
5. Mediterranean Sea, including its marginal seas, such as the Aegean Sea.
6. Persian Gulf.
7. Red Sea.

In Colonial times, sailors following the the Clipper Ship Tea Route went through seven seas near the Dutch East Indies: The Banda Sea, the Celebes Sea, the Flores Sea, the Java Sea, the South China Sea, the Sulu Sea, and the Timor Sea. It was the longest trade route in the world.

So, if someone had sailed the Seven Seas it meant he had sailed to, and then back from, the other side of the world.

Shanty, Chanty, etc.

Songs sung by sailors, pirates, and men who worked at the wharves.

"Shanties were labour songs sung by sailors of the merchant service only while at work, and never by way of recreation. Moreover—at least, in the nineteenth century—they were never used aboard men-o'-war, where all orders were carried out in silence to the pipe of the bo'sun's whistle." – from The Shanty Book, Part I, Sailor Shanties, by Richard Runciman Terry (1921)

Also, a shanty is a small hut at or near the beach.

Sheet

A rope or chain fastened to one or both the lower corners of a sail.

Ship's bell

A bell, usually on the main deck. It is the traditional method of marking time and the crew's watches.

Shiver me timbers, Shiver my timbers

Expressing surprise, and perhaps disappointment. Since the early 18th century, "shive" meant a splinter of wood. To shiver meant to break into small pieces or splinters, or to shake in the wind, and – in a nautical setting – possibly causing damage to the wood of the ship.

The expression sometimes meant the shattering of timbers when enemy vessels met, and one fired upon the other so the mast or other timbers were blown to bits.

Show a leg!

Get out of your bed (or hammock) and start doing something.

Six-water grog

> A beverage given as a punishment for neglect or drunkenness, instead of the usual four-water, which is one part rum, and four parts water, lime-juice, and sugar.

Skedaddle

> To stray or slip quietly away from a fight or a battle, without giving notice to your party.

A shot across the bow, a shot across the bows

> A shot of warning, literally or figuratively.

Skelp

> Slap with an open hand.

Sky-sail

> A small sail above the royal. Rare.

Sky-scraper

> A triangular sail set above the skysail; if square it would be a moonsail, and if set above that, a star-gazer, etc. Used in light winds on a few ships.

Slack

> The part of a rope or sail that hangs loose.

Slush

The fat of the boiled, salted beef and pork meat in the coppers, formerly the perquisite of the ship's cook.

The resulting grease could be used on board, and was often sold or traded on board the ship.

A slush bucket was kept to grease the masts, sheets, etc., to make all run smoothly.

A slush fund was money earned by the cook, from selling the slush on board, or sold in barrels when the ship made port.

Also, snow in a thaw. Any wet dirt.

Smart, Smartly

Brisk, vigorous, or sharp. To do something quickly, precisely, and without hesitation.

Snarly-yow

Someone who grumbles.

Spanish Main

The New World territories – especially the Americas – controlled by Spain in the 16th century. This included everything from the southern tip of South America, up through Central America and Mexico, then splitting east to the Atlantic ocean and west to what is now northern California.

Son of a gun

Described a boy born at sea to a sailor whose wife or other female companion was allowed to accompany him on the ship. Sometimes said with mild derision.

Sprog

A child or lively young man, usually a raw recruit.

Squadron

A relatively small detachment of soldiers or a few warships (ten or less). Usually said in a derogatory tone, considering them easy to defeat.

Squiffy

19th century expression for drunk. Can also mean someone who acts silly or stupid.

Starboard

When you're on deck facing the front of the ship, starboard is the right-hand side.

Stern

The rear part of a ship

Swab, Swabber, Swabbie

A swab is a sort of long mop, often made from strands of rope-yarn and a stick, used for cleaning the ship's decks. A swabber – sometimes just "a swab" or "a swabbie" is the person whose job it is to clean the deck. (A sea-swabber is someone lazy who does nothing of use.) This term has been used since the mid-17th century. "Swabbie" can be used affectionately or with slight derision for anyone young or new to the crew.

Swaggy

Describes an enemy's ship that's filled with plunder. Usually, an intended target.

Swash

A sudden surge in the sea.

Swashbuckling

Fighting on the high seas. To "swashbuckle" is to strike an enemy's shield with your sword.

Sweating the purser

To waste supplies.

Sweet trade

Another name for a pirate's work, but especially that of a buccaneer.

Swell

A rolling wave which seldom breaks. Causes steady heaving of a ship, even when there's no wind.

Swill

To drink greedily. Also, rank liquid.

T

Tack

> To go about, to change the course from one board
> to another from the starboard to the
> port tack, or vice versa. Accomplished by turning
> the ship's head into the wind, then falling back to
> the other side, and so on.

Taffia, Tafia

> Originally, a harsh forerunner of rum, made from
> fermented sugarcane juice, and praised for its
> medicinal value.

> Today, this is a very sweet beverage made with
> one part fruit syrup (made with fruit juice, sugar,
> and water, boiled until it starts to thicken), one
> part white rum, and garnished with additional,
> fresh fruit.

> In the 20th century, it could also refer to a
> beverage made with grenadine and a carbonated
> beverage like tonic water, or a similar non-
> alcoholic drink served in a wine or apertif glass.

Taken aback

> When the wind blows into the sails 'backwards',
> causing a sudden shift in the sails. Can be
> dangerous. Definitely slows progress.

Taking the wind out of his sails

> Steal the wind of another ship. Overbear.

Talk Like a Pirate Day

> Since 1995, celebrating pirate history, lore, legends and fun by talking like a pirate for one day: September 19th. Created by the combined geniuses of John Baur (Ol' Chumbucket) and Mark Summers (Cap'n Slappy). The day embraces the romanticized view of the Golden Age of Piracy, and associated language.
>
> It's also the only holiday that's resulted from a sports injury.
>
> Pastafarians and the Church of the Flying Spaghetti Monster celebrate Talk Like a Pirate Day as a religious holiday. According to Pastafarian beliefs, pirates are "absolute divine beings" and the original Pastafarians. Further, in Pastafarian Bobby Henderson's open letter to the Kansas School Board, he explained that "global warming, earthquakes, hurricanes, and other natural disasters are a direct effect of the shrinking numbers of pirates since the 1800s."

Tall ship

> A phrase among the early voyagers for square-rigged vessels having top-masts.

Tantara

> Noise of a drum.

Tar and feather

>A punishment for theft, first ordered by Richard I. Inflicted by stripping the delinquent, then smearing him with tar, covering him with flocks and feathers, and towing him ashore.

Tarry-breeks

>A sailor. The phrase comes from the use of tar on a ship, and from "breeks" meaning trousers. Hence, a sailor might have tar on his trousers, or tarry breeks.

Tartar

>A stern or domineering captain or commanding officer.

Tasking

>To examine a ship to see if she's seaworthy and her timbers are still sound. Routinely done after capturing an enemy vessel, before deciding what to do with it.

Tattoo

>Music – in the early days of pirates, most often a drum – signaling the end of the day. Then, after roll call (if any), the crew – except the night watch – retire for the night.

Taut hand

>Strict disciplinarian, not quite a Tartar. Example: "The cap'n, he runs th' ship wi' a right taut hand."

Tea-waggon

> Nickname for ships of the East India Company, since so many of them carried tea.

Th'

> Replaces the word "the" when you can slur the words together or say it so it's not far removed from "duh"... except not in a stupid way. At other times, when it punctuates or adds flair to your speech, you'll say "the" like "thee," so it has a sharp punch to it. "Th' lady" can be an aside or said with a touch of reverence, but – in other situations -- "the lady," said with a good stretch sounding like "thee lay-dee," it has the right sarcastic edge to it.

Thar

> There, indicating location.

Them

> Sometimes used instead of "they" or "those." Usually used with singular verbs ("them is," etc.). Example: "Them's jus' swabbies, mateys. Leave 'em be." Or, "Them be right fine jewels yer sportin', ma'am, an' prolly a might bit heavy on ye, too."

Thieves' cat

> A cat o' nine tails with knots at the end, used exclusively for punishing thieves.

Three sheets to the wind, Three sheets in the wind

> Sails (especially square sails) were secured with ropes or chains, sometimes called "sheets," to keep them from fluttering, flapping and blowing out of control in a strong wind. If three sheets were loose, the ship could be buffeted and lurch off course.
>
> Since the mid-17th century, and perhaps earlier, the expression also means drunk.
>
> Similar to the expression, "both sheets aft."

Thundering

> Adjective usually meaning powerful, excellent, fine, or good, but it can also be a modifier meaning "more." So, something could be "thundering good," or – less often – "thundering bad." To just say "Thundering!" usually indicates approval.

Ticket

> An official warrant of discharge from the Navy, may also include a reference to the sum owed to him as back pay. These were often forged, forcing the Navy to create a duplicate copy of each one, and guard the blanks.

Tie-for-tye

> A mutual agreement and exchange of equal work.

Tight

> A ship is tight when no water leaks in. (When a rope or chain is secured tightly, that's called taut.)
>
> Also a word for tipsy or drunk,

Titivate

> Early 19th century term meaning to clean up, put the finishing touches on, or to spruce up. (It's a great word to baffle people who have yet to learn to talk like a pirate. Say "It's time to go titivate!" and people will pause and blink.)

Timoneer

> Person who steers the ship. Sometimes the helmsman plus a lookout.

Tin-potter

> Someone who avoids work by pretending to be ill or injured, but seems fit enough to linger around the galley, looking for extra food.

Togs

> Clothes.

Tom Pepper

> A liar. The original Tom Pepper was, according to folklore, such a big liar that he was kicked out of Hell.

Ton for ton and man for man

>When two or more ships sail together, agreeing to fairly divide the plunder.

Trelawney

>A dish of barley meal, water and salt, or barley bread boiled in water, served when there's nothing else to eat.

Trick

>A period of time spent at the helm or wheel ("my trick's over"). Also called a spell.

Trim

>Exactly how a ship is set in the water. To trim is to set the sails so the ship gets the best of the wind.

Troacher, or Troaker

>A smuggler.

Truce

>A signal, usually by flag, to cease hostilities so a discussion (or parley) might lead to a mutual agreement.

Trying the range

>A lubberly mode of estimating the distance of an enemy's ship or fort by firing a shot at it.

Turkey-grain

>Maize, or corn.

Turn the hands up

>Summon everyone on deck.

U - V - W

Unclaimed, as Derelict

> When a ship is found with no one and no animal
> alive, on board, it's considered a good prize.
> When the Royal Navy found such a ship, they'd
> wait 366 days for it to be claimed, and then half
> the value was given to whomever had found the
> ship.
>
> When a pirate finds a ship like this, he's more
> direct in laying claim to it.

Under sail

> When a ship is making progress across the water,
> due to wind in her sails.

Under the weather

> Serving a watch on the weather side of the ship,
> exposed to wind and spray.

Under-masted

> When a ships masts are too short or too small to
> spread the sails enough to make good speed.

Union down

> When a British ship is in distress or in mourning,
> the flag is flown upside-down. When a pirate sees
> this, his reaction is at his own discretion. (The
> phrase "easy mark" comes to mind.)

Unrove his life line

> Departed this mortal world.

Up anchor!

> The anchor has been lifted. Every man to his station!

Upper deck

> The highest of those decks which are continued throughout the whole length of a ship without falls or interruptions.

Utlaghe

> Outlaw. (The word could be said to sound similar, "UHT-lahh.")

Variables

> The parts of the ocean where steady winds are unlikely and not expected.

Vessels

> The general name for any type of conveyance such as a ship, boat, etc., that can traverse the waters of the ocean, sea, rivers, etc.

Vetayle

> Food, victuals, provisions. (Vetayles can be pronounced similar to "vitals.")

Victualler

> A ship designated to carry provisions. The phrase was used as early as the 16th century, and perhaps earlier. Depending on the quality of those provisions, this could be a good prize for pirates. Such ships sometimes carried fewer crew members and less armaments for defense.

Voluntary stranding

> The practice of deliberately running a ship aground or beaching it, to avoid greater danger.

Voyage

> A journey by sea. The trip out and the trip home are each (individually) called passages.

Waif

> Goods found and not claimed. Derelict.

Waiving amain

> A salutation of defiance. Typically, brandishing weapons or firing on a ship without warning.

Walk the plank

> Part legend and perhaps part fact, when a prisoner on a ship was forced to walk, bound and blindfolded, along a board that extended outward from the deck of the ship. In most cases, the person fell into the sea and drowned. (Also see Pedro-a-pied.)

Watch

> The hours when part of the crew is at work and at their posts. A sailor is usually on duty during four-hour shifts. These hours are usually marked by the ringing of a bell.

> Though no seaman should fall asleep while on watch, if an officer does so, it's a crime punishable by death.

Water-logged

> When a ship is full of water but does not sink, due to the buoyancy of her cargo. This can be very dangerous because the ship's center of gravity can shift. Sometimes the ship can be pumped out. At other times, it must be abandoned.

> If the cargo is timber, a water-logged ship can float for a very long time.

Water spout

> A large mass of water collected in a vertical column, and moving rapidly along the surface of the sea. As contact with one has been supposed dangerous, it has been suggested to fire cannon at them.

Wave

> A volume of water rising in surges above the general level, and elevated in proportion to the wind.

Waveson

Goods floating on the waves after a shipwreck, considered derelict. Also known as flotsam or flotson.

Weather side

Side of a ship exposed to the wind.

Weigh anchor

To begin lifting the anchor from the sea bed. Once it has cleared the ground, the ship can begin moving through the water, under way.

Wench

A female, usually a young woman. Attractive but approachable.

Wend a course

Sail steadily in one direction.

Wharf, or Quay (pronounced "key")

A wood or stone platform or structure, raised on the shore -- usually at a harbor – for the convenience of loading or discharging vessels.

Whirlwind

A revolving, circular current of wind of small diameter that rises suddenly, and then vanishes quickly.

White horses

> Waves with foam or spray on the tops, usually resulting from a strong wind.

White-tape

> A smuggler's term for gin.

Wi' a wannion, With a wannion (waniron, wenion)

> 16th century phrase, perhaps older, meaning with a vengeance. (Phrase used in Shakespeare's play, Pericles, Prince of Tyre.)

-wich

> Name of a place with a harbor, such as Harwich, Greenwich, and so on.

Wicket

> A small door in the gate of a fortress, intended for access by people who travel on foot. When that door is stuck and difficult to pass through, it could be a sticky wicket.

> Also a term for the structure a batter aims at in a game of cricket, or (later) one of several hoops in the U.S. game of croquet.

Wide berth

> To leave room between two ships moored (berthed) to allow space for maneuver. In slang, to give someone the wide berth is to allow him or her lots of room, or generally avoid.

Windbound

> When a ship is detained by contrary winds and cannot move.

Windlass

> A winch used to hoist (pull up) the anchor.

Windward

> On the side that the wind is coming from.

Wishy-washy

> An alcoholic beverage that's been diluted too much with water.

> "His food the land-crab, lizard, or the frog;
> His drink a wish-wash of six-water grog." –
> Source unknown.

Woolders

> Bandages.

Working up

> Punishing members of the crew by keeping them on duty and performing insignificant tasks.

Y - Z

Yard

> The horizontal spar from which a square sail is suspended.

Yardarm

> The very end of a yard, on either side of the mast beyond the battens, usually fitted with rings or sheave-holes.

Yarn spinning

> Telling at tale or making up a story. The story is called a yarn.

Yaw

> When a ship isn't under control or is badly steered, and it turns quickly from right to left.

Yo-ho-ho, Yoe-ho-ho

> A pirate's laugh. "Yo-ho" was first an exclamation (like "Ahoy!") to attract attention, and sometimes used in place of "yo-heave-ho" (or yoe-heave-ho) to coordinate sailors' efforts to haul something in.

Zig-zag course

> Using very short tacks to work the ship windward.

A Brief History of Pirates

Piracy – from the Latin, *pirata,* a rogue or someone who plots -- is loosely defined as robbery and plunder, or criminal violence at sea. We like to think of it in happier terms. However, piracy has certainly had a checkered past.

Pirates have existed for centuries, possibly as far back as time is recorded. Piracy, as we use the word, probably began in the eastern Mediterranean.

In the fourteenth century BC, the Lukka were pirates off the coast of Asia Minor. In addition to raiding Cyprus, they targeted Egyptian ships.

Around 3000 BC, Sumerians – especially those near the Tigris and Euphrates Rivers – were steadily under attack by pirates.

Then, in the second millennium BC, the Sea Peoples (or Peoples of the Sea) came from places unknown and began raiding in the Mediterranean. They targeted Egypt during the 19th and 20th dynasties, especially during the eras of Ramesses II, Merneptah, and Ramesses III. It's believed that they eventually settled around modern-day Palestine and were the ancestors of the Philistines and the maritime trading culture known as the Phoenicians.

After that, Crete became well-known for the pirates who used it as a base for about 800 years.

Even Julius Caesar was captured by pirates when he was on a trip to Rhodes in 78 BC. After his ransom was paid, Caesar swore to return for revenge. Soon after that, he returned with four ships and about 500 men, and crucified every pirate not killed in the attack.

About 10 years later, not to be outdone, Pompey launched a huge anti-pirate campaign, killing over 10,000 pirates around the Cilician sea, including Illyrian pirates.

The earliest pirate whose name survives might be Anicetus, from around modern Turkey. He was active in an anti-Roman uprising, and died around 69 AD.

After the fall of the Roman Empire and the sacking of Constantinople (1204 AD), the Aegean Sea reigned as one of the most notorious homes for pirates. Within about 100 years, they'd been subdued by the Muslim Ottoman Empire.

From the 8th to the 12th century, some regard Vikings as the leading pirates of the day. A lot depends on how you define "pirates," since many of their attacks were land-based more than at sea. Whether you use the p-word or not, Vikings certainly terrorized most of Europe.

By the late 15th century, Barbary pirates were using North Africa as a base, mostly Algiers, Tunis, and Tripoli. From there, they attacked ships in the Mediterranean. They were soon under the attack of the Knights of Malta, who – in turn – raided a variety of areas (including Venice, infuriating the Pope) until Napoleon subdued them in 1798.

By the end of the 15th century, European countries did not have the manpower to subdue increasing pirate activity on the high seas. The British Admiralty decided to authorize the East India Company – already under attack from pirates – to deal with pirates by any means necessary. Generally, this meant hanging, branding on the forehead with the letter P, or flogging. In some cases, that deterred pirate attacks, but not completely.

The 16th century brought the development of large-scale sailing ships equipped with cannon. That led to a dramatic increase in colonization. However, until the 17th century, navies were rarely well-organized for the purposes of defense at sea. In most cases, pirates could still attack with impunity.

The Spanish Main was among the pirate targets of the 16th century. The Spanish Main included all the territories in the Americas that had been seized by the Spanish, from the tip of South America, through Central America, and splitting east to the Atlantic and west to what we now call northern California.

The formal practice of *privateering* – piracy conducted with licenses (especially Letters of Marque) from governments – also emerged in the 17th century. With authority and sometimes funding by various countries, including England, France, and Spain, privateers left port armed and ready to attack ships from enemy countries.

It's often joked that privateers honored the Letter of Marque, but pirates kept the loot themselves. In all other respects, many of them operated in similar manners.

The time from the middle of the 17th century through about 1730 is called the Golden Age of Piracy.

Through the latter half of the 18th century, piracy declined due to several factors. One was the increased ability of European governments to patrol the seas. In 1830, the French invaded Algiers, which meant the end to most corsair (Mediterranean pirates) activities.

However, natural disasters struck as well. In 1692, the pirate have of Port Royal (Jamaica) was almost leveled by an earthquake, killing over 2000 people, many (or most) of them pirates.

And, in general, times were changing. Dramatic social changes began with the successful revolution in America, forming the United States, and the revolution that followed in France. Then, exploration and development in the Americas attracted adventurers just as piracy once did.

By the middle of the 19th century, privateers and pirates were generally outlawed.

Of course, piracy – as originally defined – continues today in uncontrolled waters near unstable nations. That's not the subject of this book.

In a created realm within modern culture, our romantic version of piracy thrives. We connect with others in pirate crews, companies and guilds. At annual events like Dragon*Con, we meet even more people who share our enthusiasm for the pirate dream.

Ours is a vision of swashbuckling pirates – men and women – with eye patches, fold-down boots, parrots, Jolly Rogers, and a hearty "Arr!" for all.

As author Frank Stockton said, "From the very earliest days of history there have been pirates, and it is, therefore, not at all remarkable that, in the early days of the history of this continent, sea-robbers should have made themselves prominent; but the buccaneers of America differed in many ways from those pirates with whom the history of the old world has made us acquainted."

And, as A. Grove Day said in *Pirates of the Pacific,* "A pirate might be called a highwayman who has taken to waylaying and looting ships." That romantic highwayman image fits well.

Most popular stories of pirates come from the Golden Age of Piracy, the 1650s to the 1730s. This is the era represented by classics from Robert Louis Stevenson's *Treasure Island* to J. M. Barrie's *Peter Pan.*

That golden age is usually divided into three eras: The time of the buccaneers, the years in which the Pirate Round became popular, and the post-Spanish Succession period.

Buccaneering Period

Though many people regard this as a pre-Golden Age time, buccaneers flourished from around 1650 to 1680. That's when buccaneers, mostly on Jamaica and Tortuga, were attacking the Spanish colonies (the Spanish Main) as well as Spanish ships in the Caribbean and eastern Pacific. As you'll learn, the buccaneers had good reasons for this.

The Pirate Round

Piracy quickly expanded during the 1690s. They followed a route opened by Vasco de Gama in the late 15th century. Pirates sailed from Bermuda and the Americas, circling around Africa by the Cape of Good Hope, then traveling north to rob ships in the Indian Ocean and at the mouth of the Red Sea. Among their favorite targets were cargo-laden ships of the East India Trading Company, which had been chartered in 1600.

For many pirates, this began as a "steal from the rich and give to the poor" venture. There were good reasons for that, as well.

However, the Pirate Round was a difficult route and perils increased as more trading ships joined convoys for protection. In addition, the War of Succession offered legal jobs that required less work and paid more reliably. So, by 1720, the Pirate Round was almost abandoned.

The Post-Spanish Succession Period

This era, from around 1716 to 1726, turned piracy into a popular career.

It started with the War of the Spanish Succession (1710 - 1714). That's when it looked like France and Spain were going to merge and form one very powerful country under a single monarch. European navies grew rapidly in response, and ship crews often included former privateers and pirates.

When that war ended, many sailors and and other recruits were suddenly unemployed. They liked the sea and they were accustomed to the independent lifestyle.

So, many turned en masse to piracy in the Caribbean, the American eastern seaboard, the West African coast, and the Indian Ocean.

At the same time, colonial settlement – especially in the Americas – meant that large quantities of valuable cargoes were being shipped across the Atlantic. Piracy could be very profitable.

So, when talking about pirates, most people think about piracy in the late 17th and early 18th centuries. However, pirates from other eras have earned popular attention, as well.

Here are a few of the most famous pirates and privateers, and the approximate years when they plied their trade as pirates.

Early and Famous

William Kyd (Not the same as Captain Kidd) 1430 - 1450
Hayreddin Pasha and Aruj Barbarossa (Redbeard) 1504 - 1545 (Two brothers, sometimes identified as one person called Barbarossa.)
Jean Fleury (Florin) 1520 - 1530 (The first to prey on Spanish ships laden with precious cargo from Montezuma.)

Sea Dogs and Corsairs

Turgut (Dragut) Reis 1520 - 1565 (Described as one of the most feared of the corsairs.)
Pedro Menéndez de Avilés 1565
Thomas Cavendish 1587 - 1592 (The first man to intentionally circumnavigate the globe.)

Sir Francis Drake 1563 - 1596 (One of the most
successful privateers in history.)
Gráinne O'Malley (Gráinne Ní Mháille, Grace O'Malley)
1560 - 1600
Sir Francis Verney 1608 - 1610
Sir Henry Mainwaring 1610 - 1616

Buccaneer Era

Anne Dieu-Le-Veut 1650 - 1704
Thomas Veal ? - 1658 (Associated with pirate treasure
still hidden at Dungeon Rock.)
Charlotte de Berry 1660 - 1670
Sir Henry Morgan 1663 - 1674 (One of Grace
O'Blarney's husband's ancestors.)
Jacques Tavernier (Le Lyonnais) 1664 - 1673

Pirate Round Era

Thomas Tew 1692 - 1695 (Among the early pioneers of
the route later known as the Pirate Round.)
William "Captain" Kidd 1695 - 1699 (Left an
undiscovered buried treasure "east of Boston," often
associated with the Oak Island Money Pit.)

Post-Spanish Succession

Blackbeard (Edward Teach) 1716 - 1718 (Left buried
treasure, also associated with Oak Island.)
Lars Gathenhielm 1710 - 1718
Ingela Gathenhielm 1718 - 1721 (Widow of Lars, who
took command of the his pirate business and even
expanded it.)
Richard Worley ? - 1719 (One of the first to fly the Jolly
Roger.)
Bartholomew Roberts (Black Bart) 1719 - 1722
Mary Read   ? - 1720

"Calico Jack" John Rackham ? - 1720 (Husband of Anne Bonny.)
William Condon ? - 1721
Anne Bonny (or Bonney) ? - 1725
Eric Cobham and Maria Lindsey 1720 - 1740 (Husband and wife.)

Later 18th and 19th Century Pirates and Privateers

George and Rachel Wall 1781 - 1782 (Husband & wife, she was hung in Boston, 1789.)
José Gaspar (Gasparilla) 1783 - 1821
Sam Hall Lord 1800 - 1840
Samuel Mason ? - 1803 (American hero of the Revolutionary War.)
Jean Lafitte 1803 - 1815, 1817 - 1821 (Hero of Battle of New Orleans.)
Pierre Lafitte 1803 - 1821 (Brother of Jean Lafitte.)
Catherine Hagerty and Charlotte Badger 1806
Benito de Soto 1827 - 1830
Bully Hayes 1850 - 1877 (Described as "the last of the buccaneers.")

As you can see, notable pirates lived in many eras, and came from many backgrounds. Most were men but plenty of them were women, and some were husband-and-wife partnerships.

Now, let's talk more about the Golden Age of Piracy, and why pirates thrived during those years.

Buccaneers

Frank R. Stockton said, in *Buccaneer and Pirates of Our Coast,*

"The buccaneers were not unlike that class of men known in our western country as cowboys. Young fellows of good families from England and France often determined to embrace a life of adventure, and possibly profit, and sailed out to the West Indies to get gold and hides, and to fight Spaniards.

"Frequently they dropped their family names and assumed others more suitable to roving freebooters, and, like the bold young fellows who ride over our western plains, driving cattle and shooting Indians, they adopted a style of dress as free and easy, but probably not quite so picturesque, as that of the cowboy.

"They soon became a very rough set of fellows, in appearance as well as action, endeavoring in every way to let the people of the western world understand that they were absolutely free and independent of the manners and customs, as well as of the laws of their native countries."

The word, *buccaneer,* eventually became synonymous with the word pirate. However, its roots were far more mundane and domestic.

The original word, *buccan,* came from the Arawak, a group of indigenous people who lived in the Caribbean, among other locations. They were the native people first encountered by Christopher Columbus in 1492. (DNA tests show that the majority of people in Puerto Rico are descendants of the Arawak.)

In the language of the Arawak, the word *buccan* indicated a wooden frame used for smoking meat. Later, the French adopted the word and spelled it *boucan* or *boucane.*

French settlers and other Europeans began settling in the Caribbean, without authorization from their respective countries. Most of those settlers were men, not families. The Arawak taught the settlers to use wooden frames to cook and smoke the meat from feral cattle (not just cows) and pigs. From that tradition, our modern-day barbecues developed.

However, Spanish conquerors drove most of those *boucaniers* from their islands to the larger island of Hispaniola (now Haiti and the Dominican Republic). In the 1630s, the Spanish were on the march again, this time driving the boucaniers from Hispaniola. Many settled in Tortuga, an island off the northwest coast of the Haiti side of Hispaniola. They were soon joined by more French, English, and Dutch settlers, and they included runaway slaves, deserters, and escaped prisoners. They united with an equal hatred of the Spanish.

Called buccaneers by the English settlers in nearby Jamaica, the migrant and dispossessed bands on Tortuga took to piracy. Generally, they used small ships and boats to attack Spanish vessels – especially galleons – in the Windward Passage, a strait between Cuba and Hispaniola.

In time, the buccaneers added a base in the Jamaican town of Port Royal, and were known as the "Brethren of the Coast." For a price, they could be hired as mercenaries, or – more politely – privateers. Since Jamaica had become a British possession, the British government often commissioned privateers to do what the buccaneers wanted to do anyway: Attack Spanish ships.

However, between paid assignments, buccaneers roamed the seas freely, attacking ships at will. Generally, but not always, they avoided ships owned by governments that paid them. Then, several pirate crews turned renegade and targeted any ship with a valuable cargo.

Though pirates plied their trade across the high seas long before and long after the buccaneer era, their time established the foundation of today's creative vision of pirates.

The Pirate Round

The Pirate Round was a general route used predominantly between 1693 and 1700 and 1719 to 1721. Pirates who followed it were sometimes called Rounders or Roundsmen.

The route generally started at or near the eastern coast of North America, mostly New York, Bermuda, and Nassau. From there, pirates pointed their ships towards the coast of Africa via the Madeiras. After rounding the Cape of Good Hope, pirates sailed to the Madagascar area to prepare for battle.

Madagascar was a haven for pirates for about 30 years. Buccaneers set up their own kingdoms among the islands, sheltering pirate ships en route the Red Sea... or anywhere else they might seize East Indian ships with rich cargoes.

On the return trip, pirates would pause around Madagascar again, either for rest and recovery, or to wait out the worst of monsoon season and sail when seas were calmer. Drinking and gambling were plentiful, so many pirates left for home with lighter pockets than they'd expected.

Around Madagascar, pirates generally favored the ports of St. Mary's (Ile Sainte-Marie) and Ranter Bay, or the nearby islands of the Comoros.

By around 1718, piracy around Madagascar was temporarily halted. Increasing protection for East Indian ships made raids less successful and profitable. In addition, many pirates had found legal (and better paying) work aboard ships involved in the War of Spanish Succession. Fewer were willing to risk their lives attacking ships in the seven seas, especially the Red Sea and the Indian Ocean. The navy offered them something better, and they took it.

Then, when the War of Spanish Succession was over, many sailors – including former pirates – found themselves jobless. Piracy resumed with fresh energy, so the Pirate Round (and Madagascar) briefly regained some popularity.

However, greater treasures awaited pirates in the Caribbean. The arduous trip and risks of the Pirate Round gradually lost their appeal as pirates looked to the Atlantic for fresh opportunities.

Post-Spanish Succession

In 1700, pirate Emmanuel Wynne was either the first – or one of the first – to fly the Jolly Roger. Pirates were becoming better organized, and better prepared for battle.

The start of the 18th century also saw a surge in pirate numbers, especially after the War of Spanish Succession. Dismissed from their positions in the navy, these men didn't want to go back to farming and servitude. Instead, they continued to work in the trade they knew best: Sailing the high seas, attacking enemy ships.

Governments increased their efforts to eliminate piracy on the high seas. For awhile, it was touch-and-go. Pirates would be cleared out of one area, and immediately double elsewhere. Briefly, it was swashbuckling at its finest.

When you see movies portraying pirates, they often reflect the flair and elegance of early 18th century buccaneers.

Then, important changes affect for those interested in adventure and profits. Land-based opportunities opened, especially in North America. Fur trading was enormously profitable, trading for beaver skins in the north and deerskins in the south, then selling them to the English for up to ten times the cost.

Rum and brandy production, as well as smuggling, were other profitable options for former pirates who wanted an easier life.

The risks were different and – for some – more attractive. The New World was expanding rapidly, and entrepreneurial opportunities improved daily.

At the same time, government resources improved. Alliances – such as the one formed in 1703 between Britain and Portugal – dramatically improved maritime defenses against piracy. During the relatively peaceful time between 1714 and the Spanish war of 1739, navies had the focus and manpower to invade pirate strongholds and capture leaders of the pirate community.

Blackbeard's pirate career lasted a scant two years before a British naval officer killed him in 1718. In 1720, noted pirates Anne Bonny, her husband Calico Jack, and Mary Read were all captured off the coast of Jamaica and found guilty of piracy. Black Bart followed in 1722.

Of course, piracy continued. The eras of Jean Lafitte and Gasparilla had not yet arrived. However, piracy's peak – the Golden Age – was declining rapidly, and declared over around 1730.

Honor among thieves

During the Golden Age of Piracy, most pirate ships had a code of conduct. Only four of those early codes are known to exist today. One of the most detailed was used by Bartholomew Roberts (Black Bart), who sailed between 1719 and 1722.

The Pirates'
Code of Conduct

According to early "pyrate" historians such as Daniel Defoe, the following is the pirates' code of Black Bart.

I. Every man has a vote in affairs of moment; has equal title to the fresh provisions, or strong liquors, at any time seized, and may use them at pleasure, unless a scarcity (not an uncommon thing among them) makes it necessary, for the good of all, to vote a retrenchment.

II. Every man to be called fairly in turn, by list, on board of prizes because, (over and above their proper share) they were on these occasions allowed a shift of clothes: but if they defrauded the company to the value of a dollar in plate, jewels, or money, marooning was their punishment.

If the robbery was only betwixt one another, they contented themselves with slitting the ears and nose of him that was guilty, and set him on shore, not in an uninhabited place, but somewhere, where he was sure to encounter hardships.

III. No person to game at cards or dice for money.

IV. The lights and candles to be put out at eight o'clock at night: if any of the crew, after that hour still remained inclined for drinking, they were to do it on the open deck

V. To keep their piece, pistols, and cutlass clean and fit for service.

VI. No boy or woman to be allowed amongst them.

If any man were to be found seducing any of the latter sex, and carried her to sea, disguised, he was to suffer death; so that when any fell into their hands, as it chanced in the Onslow, they put a sentinel immediately over her to prevent ill consequences from so dangerous an instrument of division and quarrel; but then here lies the roguery; they contend who shall be sentinel, which happens generally to one of the greatest bullies, who, to secure the lady's virtue, will let none lie with her but himself.

VII. To desert the ship or their quarters in battle, was punished with death or marooning.

VIII. No striking one another on board, but every man's quarrels to be ended on shore, at sword and pistol.

The quarter-master of the ship, when the parties will not come to any reconciliation, accompanies them on shore with what assistance he thinks proper, and turns the disputant back to back, at so many paces distance; at the word of command, they turn and fire immediately, (or else the piece is knocked out of their hands). If both miss, they come to their cutlasses, and then he is declared the victor who draws the first blood.

IX. No man to talk of breaking up their way of living, till each had shared one thousand pounds. If in order to this, any man should lose a limb, or become a cripple in their service, he was to have eight hundred dollars, out of the public stock, and for lesser hurts, proportionately.

X. The captain and quartermaster to receive two shares of a prize:the master, boatswain, and gunner, one share and a half, and other officers one and quarter.

XI. The musicians to have rest on the Sabbath Day, but the other six days and nights, none without special favour.

Pirate Costuming
and Character Notes

The best approach to pirate garb with flair is to decide your character ahead of time. Consider where he or she is from, the character's era, class level and budget, and idiosyncrasies.

Choosing a character

Clothing (including garb and costuming) says a lot about a person, and that's especially true when you're playing a role or representing a pirate persona.

If you're highly creative and industrious, you can start with a unique character that you create. In writing books and online, you can find character archetypes to start with. (Online, search using terms like "writing character archetypes." Typically, you'll start with a list like the Motivator, Actor, Inventor, Promoter, Entertainer, Wizard, Mentor, Detective, and so on. Then, you'll refine that, including the idiosyncrasies that suit you and make your persona unique.

Of course, pirate movies – especially the classics starring people like Errol Flynn and Douglas Fairbanks (Sr. and Jr.) – already include archetypical pirates. You could watch those and choose a persona. Then, add and embellish more characteristics based on one or more other characters. (More recent formula movies, including *Swashbucker, Cuthroat Island,* the *Pirates of the Caribbean* series, and even *Muppet Treasure Island* can be very good, too. See Wikipedia's List of pirate films by year.)

Remember, you're starting with archetypes. They'll give you a familiar foundation to start with.

Cast a broader net with movies and TV series such as *Robin Hood, Merlin,* and *Farscape.* You'll see characters that loosely fit traditional archetypes, but they'll give you even more latitude for crafting your own pirate persona.

Once you've chosen the basic elements of your character, fine-tune it with a personal history. For example, your persona's country, education and economic background will affect your accent and vocabulary, your manners, and the clothing you're comfortable in plus what you put on to impress others.

The more you understand your character or persona, the easier it is to add clothing that conveys exactly who you are, on sight.

Costuming and garb, in general and by gender

Pirates did not have uniforms. Often, their garb represented their homeland or at least their last ports of call.

Most pirates were men, so pirate garb is most reliably described in terms of what men wore. That's what we're focusing on in this chapter.

However, some pirates were women. In fact, in the book *Seafaring Women,* author David Cordingly comments about a prevalent belief that water is a female element, and that women hold a unique power over the sea.

He also quotes Pliny's *Natural History* (77 AD), in which he said, "... out at sea, a storm may be lulled by a woman uncovering her body." So, women might be aboard a pirate ship – if not an actual pirate, herself – during any time in pirate history.

While women have the option of wearing skirts and shoes with higher heels, they're not limited to them. For reasons of practicality, many female pirates wore men's garb. Some women concealed their gender, at least initially. And, especially in the buccaneer era, men and women both wore lace trim on their clothing.

Of course, modern pirates can choose from an eclectic mix of styles covering many pirate eras, adapted to his or her personal style. From faerie pirates to Steampunk pirates, there are no limits, except as imposed by the rules of your crew, company, or guild.

Wardrobe and accessories

For a basic pirate wardrobe, just a few accents can convey the look. They could include an eye patch, the obligatory gold hoop earring, and at least one kind of weapon represented. A head scarf or bandeau, plus a soft-brimmed hat, also send the message that you're a pirate.

Torn-off trousers and a rope belt could work, especially if – as Tom Lichtenheld suggested in *Everything I Know about Pirates* – your trousers look like they been bitten by sharks.

A wide waist sash or cummerbund is a good extra. Opulent accessories include a flowing cloak (see Geoffrey Holder's in the 1976 movie, *Swashbuckler*) and some kind of bucket-top or folded-down boots.

No matter how authentic or anachronistic your look, accessories can make or break the impression you create.

Note: If you're wearing knee breeches, make sure your knees are always covered. If your thigh-high or over-the-knee socks and stockings tend to droop, shop for modified and concealed sock garters made for men. You can find them in styles designed to be worn at thigh level.

Here are costuming notes from each of four centuries of piracy, from the 16th through the 19th centuries.

Corsairs

For a pirate in the corsairs style, think about Aladdin. Since most of these pirates were Muslims, a turban is a nice, authentic option. Choose harem pants with a cummerbund or waist sash, short jackets, simple shirts, and several glistening weapons.

If you're mixing cultural references, remember that the 16th century included the eras of Henry VIII and Elizabeth I.

Buccaneers

Buccaneers were originally Europeans who'd settled illegally in the Caribbean. Because their diet included lots of barbecued meat, their clothing was often made from the leather of the animals they slaughtered for food. So, if you're aiming for authenticity and you're representing an actual buccaneer (*boucanier*), all of your clothing should be made from leather or faux leather.

However... buccaneers are usually represented in clothing styled after European Cavaliers. They wore full-skirted jackets, and loose, poet-style shirts, sometimes with wide, lace-edged collars. They might wear knee-length breeches with high waistlines, and bucket-topped (folded down) boots or buckle-style shoes with knee stockings.

For historical references, see the elegant garb of the court of Charles I.

Post-Spanish Succession

Representing pirates of this era, look at clothing from Colonial America, especially the early years. Frock coats, breeches, shoes with buckles, tricorn-style hats, and big shirts with deep cuffs are typical for this era of piracy. A cravat can be worn, but the general impression should be elegant and more hip and modern than your buccaneer counterparts. In the early 18th century, lines were cleaner, simpler, and tidier.

For women not dressing as men, portraits of Molly Pitcher represent the practical clothing of women who worked alongside men.

However, some pirates continued to dress in finery from an earlier era. Black Bart (Bartholomew Roberts, active from 1719 - 1722), was buried in his signature crimson red coat and breeches with a matching feather in his hat.

Later 18th and 19th centuries

By the late 19th century, pirates could dress as over-the-top as the courtiers of George III, or more simply as his son George, Prince of Wales (the Prince Regent, later George IV) and neighboring trend-setter, France's Emperor Napoleon.

Think in terms of Darcy from Pride and Prejudice. That's the fashion of the early 19th century. In general, only the older generation wore powdered wigs and heavy makeup (for men and women).

Since our era of piracy was mostly over by the middle of the 19th century, anything Victorian is too recent for accuracy, unless you're adopting an anachronistic style like Steampunk.

Remember, Letters of Marque and Reprisal were outlawed in European countries in 1856, ending the privateer era, and – with it – much of the romantic pirate era, as well.

However, even if you're choosing a traditional pirate persona, you can still represent a pirate from the later 19th century. For example, if you're representing 19th century pirates in the South Seas or from around the Philippines, costuming can range from tropical to exotic... probably mixed with some traditional pirate garb, as well.

In terms of characters, remember that pirates came from all walks of life, and several (perhaps many) pirate captains were from the upper class. So, it's fine to work with whatever resources you have, and whatever character you'd like to create. As long as an aspiring crew member agreed to the Code of Conduct, background and wardrobe didn't necessarily matter.

And, you'll never go wrong by emulating something you saw in the Pirates of the Caribbean movies.

A Note about Parrots and Pirates

A real or fake parrot on your shoulder can really seal your identity as an authentic pirate (or someone who aspires to be one). It's the stereotypical accessory.

Many people think that author Robert Louis Stevenson created the association of parrots and pirates, out of his imagination. In *Treasure Island,* he mentions Captain Flint, the green parrot owned by Long John Silver:

"The parrot sat, preening her plumage, on Long John's shoulder."

However, pirate captain William Dampier (1651 - 1715) mentioned parrots long before Robert Louis Stevenson did. Apparently, they were considered valuable cargo for the high prices that parrots could bring, back in Europe. In Dampier's diary he said:

"The tame Parrots we found here were the largest and fairest Birds of their kind that I ever saw in the West Indies. Their colour was yellow and red, very coursly mixt; and they would prate very prettily; and there was scarce a Man but what sent aboard one or two of them. So that with Provision, Chests, Hencoops and Parrot-Cages, our Ships were full of Lumber, with which we intended to sail."

And, in his journal, *A Voyage to New Holland, etc.,* in the year1699, Dampier said:

"Here are also kept tame monkeys, parrots, parakeets, etc, which the seamen carry home."

I'm not certain that a parakeet or a monkey would convey the same impression of authenticity as a parrot. A lot depends on how much flair you bring to the persona.

For more information about costuming and characters, visit our website, http://TalkLikeAPirate.org

Pirate Songs and Shanties

No self-respecting pirate would consider his or her persona complete without knowing a few pirate songs or shanties.

Some historians maintain that authentic sea shanty (or shantie, chanty, chantie) is a single line, spontaneously made up and sung, followed by a chorus like the following:

'Blow a man down is a blow me down trick.
Blow – Blow – Blow – a man Down.
Blow a man down to the home of old Nick.
Give me some time to blow a man down.'

The classic pirate song is, of course, *15 Men on a Dead Man's Chest* (Yo-ho-ho and a Bottle of Rum). It was popularized as the song, *Derelict,* in the 1901 musical, *Treasure Island.* The lyrics were by Young E. Allison, who'd written the poem years earlier.

This was sung by the *Treasure Island* character, Billy Bones.

Fifteen men on the dead man's chest --
Yo-ho-ho and a bottle of rum!
Drink and the devil had done for the rest --
Yo-ho-ho and a bottle of rum!
    *   *   *   *   *
Fifteen men on the dead man's chest--
Yo-ho-ho and a bottle of rum!
Drink and the devil had done for the rest --
Yo-ho-ho and a bottle of rum!
The mate was fixed by the bos'n's pike,
The bos'n brained with a marlinspike

And Cookey's throat was marked belike
    It had been gripped
      By fingers ten;
    And there they lay,
      All good dead men,
Like break-o'-day in a boozing-ken --
    Yo-ho-ho and a bottle of rum!
    *   *   *   *   *

Fifteen men of a whole ship's list --
    Yo-ho-ho and a bottle of rum!
Dead and bedamned, and the rest gone whist! --
    Yo-ho-ho and a bottle of rum!
The skipper lay with his nob in gore
Where the scullion's axe his cheek had shore --
And the scullion he was stabbed times four.
    And there they lay,
      And the soggy skies
    Dripped all day long
      In up-staring eyes --
At murk sunset and at foul sunrise --
    Yo-ho-ho and a bottle of rum!
    *   *   *   *   *

Fifteen men of 'em stiff and stark --
    Yo-ho-ho and a bottle of rum!
Ten of the crew had the Murder mark --
    Yo-ho-ho and a bottle of rum!
'Twas a cutlass swipe, or an ounce of lead,
    Or a yawing hole in a battered head --
And the scuppers glut with a rotting red.
    And there they lay --
      Aye, damn my eyes! --
    All lookouts clapped
      On paradise --
All souls bound just contrariwise --
    Yo-ho-ho and a bottle of rum!
    *   *   *   *   *

Fifteen men of 'em good and true --

Yo-ho-ho and a bottle of rum!
Every man jack could ha' sailed with Old Pew --
   Yo-ho-ho and a bottle of rum!
There was chest on chest full of Spanish gold,
With a ton of plate in the middle hold,
And the cabins riot of stuff untold.
      And they lay there
         That had took the plum,
      With sightless glare
         And their lips struck dumb,
While we shared all by the rule of thumb --
   Yo-ho-ho and a bottle of rum!
      *   *   *   *   *
More was seen through the sternlight screen --
   Yo-ho-ho and a bottle of rum!
Chartings ondoubt where a woman had been --
   Yo-ho-ho and a bottle of rum!
A flimsy shift on a bunker cot,
With a thin dirk slot through the bosom spot
And the lace stiff-dry in a purplish blot.
      Or was she wench ...
         Or some shuddering maid...?
      That dared the knife
         And that took the blade!
By God! she was stuff for a plucky jade --
   Yo-ho-ho and a bottle of rum!
      *   *   *   *   *
Fifteen men on the dead man's chest --
   Yo-ho-ho and a bottle of rum!
Drink and the devil had done for the rest --
   Yo-ho-ho and a bottle of rum!
We wrapped 'em all in a mains'l tight,
With twice ten turns of a hawser's bight,
And we heaved 'em over and out of sight--
      With a yo-heave-ho!
         And a fare-you-well!
      And a sullen plunge

In the sullen swell
Ten fathoms deep on the road to hell --
    Yo-ho-ho and a bottle of rum!
        *   *   *   *   *

Abel Brown is a more body song among pirate shanty classics. It's traditional and its origins are unknown. A variation, *Barnacle Bill the Sailor,* was popularized in entertainment and cartoons such as the *Popeye* series.

Abel Brown, the Sailor

Oh, where am I goin' to sleep tonight?
Sez Abel Brown the sailor.
You can sleep upon a mat,
Cried the fair young maiden.

2. Oh, the mat is rough, an' my skin ain't tough,
Sez Abel Brown the sailor.
You can sleep upon the shelf,
Cried the fair young maiden.

3. What 'ave you got upon the shelf?
Sez Abel Brown the sailor.
I've got some rum upon the shelf,
Cried the fair young maiden.

4. Me throat is long, an' me thirst is strong,
Sez Abel Brown the sailor.
What if you roll from off the shelf?
Cried the fair young maiden.

5. I'll bounce on the floor an' ask for more,
Sez Abel Brown the sailor.
What if police should come to the house?
Cried the fair young maiden.

6. I'll take 'em on in two's or three's,
Sez Abel Brown the sailor.
Then I'll let you stay with me,
Cried the fair young maiden.

Bibliography

"Abel Brown, the Sailor." Musica International. The Virtual Choral Library, n.d. Web. 03 Aug. 2012. <http://www.musicanet.org/robokopp/shanty/abelbrow.htm>.

Bonanos, Christopher. "Did Pirates Really Say 'Arrrr'?" Slate. N.p., n.d. Web. 03 Aug. 2012. <http://www.slate.com/articles/news_and_politics/explainer/2 007/06/did_pirates_really_say_arrrr.html>.

Carlin, J. W., ed. A Naval Encyclopædia: Comprising a Dictionary of Nautical Words and Phrases; Biographical Notices, and Records of Naval Officers; Special Articles of Naval Art and Science. Philadelphia: L. R. Hamersly & Co., 1890. Print.

Carpenter, John Reeve. Pirates - Scourge of the Seas. New York: Barnes & Noble, 2006. Print.

Cordingly, David. Seafaring Women - Adventures of Pirate Queens, Female Stowaways, and Sailors' Wives. New York: Random House, 2001. Print.

Day, A. Grove. Pirates of the Pacific. New York: Meredith Press, 1968. Print.

Defoe, Daniel. "A General History of the Pyrates." Eastern North Carolina Digital Library. East Carolina University, n.d. Web. 09 Aug. 2012. <http://digital.lib.ecu.edu/historyfiction/item.aspx?id=joh>.

Eric, Cap'n, trans. "Nautical Terms." Official International be Talkin Like a Pirate Day for Down Undaaaaarrrr. N.p., n.d. Web. 03 Aug. 2012. <http://rrr.yaaarrr.com/node/8>.

Evans, Lisa, and Robert Traynor. "The Pimpernel Phrase Book." Blakeney Manor - Home of the Scarlet Pimpernell. N.p., n.d. Web. 04 Aug. 2012. <http://www.blakeneymanor.com/phrase.html>.

Haigh, Ted. "Rediscovering Vintage Cocktails: Meet the Sangaree." Imbibe - Liquid Culture. Imbibe magazine, n.d. Web. 06 Aug. 2012. <http://www.imbibemagazine.com/The-History-of-Sangaree-Cocktails>.

Heckman, Richard, ed. Yankees Under Sail. Dublin: Yankee Books, 1968. Print.

Henderson, Bobby. "Open Letter to Kansas School Board." Church of the Flying Spaghetti Monster. N.p., 2005. Web. 09 Aug. 2012. <http://Open Letter To Kansas School Board>.

Houghton, Sally, ed. "Regency Cant and Expressions." Georgette Heyer. N.p., n.d. Web. 06 Aug. 2012. <http://www.georgette-heyer.com/slang.html>.

"International Talk Like a Pirate Day." Wikipedia. N.p., n.d. Web. 03 Aug. 2012. <http://en.wikipedia.org/wiki/International_Talk_Like_a_Pirat e_Day>. This is one of several useful historical and pirate references at Wikipedia, used as research starting-points for this book.

Knights, Edward M. "Navigation Before Netscape." History Magazine. N.p., Oct. 2001. Web. 03 Aug. 2012. <http://www.history-magazine.com/navigation.html>.

Krause, Staci Rosethorn. "A Pirate's Vocabulary." Puzzle Pirates. N.p., n.d. Web. 04 Aug. 2012. <http://www.puzzlepirates.com/Vocabulary.xhtml>.

Lichetenheld, Tom. Everything I Know about Pirates. New York: Simon & Schuster, 2000. Print.

Lincoln, Margarette. The Pirate's Handbook. New York: Cobblehill Books, 1995. Print.

Little, William, comp. The Oxford Universal Dictionary on Historical Principles. London: Oxford at the Clarendon Press, 1955. Print.

Martin, Gary. "Nautical Phrases." The Phrase Finder. N.p., n.d. Web. 03 Aug. 2012. <http://www.phrases.org.uk/meanings/nautical-phrases.html>.

Maynard, Christopher. Pirates! Raiders of the High Seas. London: Dorling Kindersley, 1998. Print. Eyewitness Readers.

Morin, Monte. "'Women and children first' is a myth." Los Angeles Times. N.p., n.d. Web. 03 Aug. 2012. <http://www.latimes.com/news/science/la-sci-sinking-ship-manners-20120731,0,197854.story>.

Palmer, Brian. "Abandoning Ship: An Etiquette Guide." Slate. N.p., n.d. Web. 03 Aug. 2012. <http://www.slate.com/articles/news_and_politics/explainer/2 012/01/costa_concordia_sinking_what_s_the_etiquette_for_a bandoning_ship_.html>.

"Parrots in History." Avian Enrichment. N.p., n.d. Web. 08 Aug. 2012.
<https://www.avianenrichment.com/fun_history.htm>.

Peacock, John. Costume 1066 - 1990s. London: Thames & Hudson, 1994. Print.

Quillen, Columbine. "Oldest Rum Cocktail – El Bumboo from 1664." Q Mix-a-Lot. N.p., 27 Feb. 2010. Web. 05 Aug. 2012. <http://qmixalot.com/oldest-rum-cocktail-el-bumboo-from-1664>.

Ross, Stewart. Pirates - Fact or Fiction. Brookfield: Copper Beech Books, 1995. Print.

Scott, Tom. "Pirate Speak: How To Talk Like A Pirate." Talk Like A Pirate Day - Official British HQ. N.p., n.d. Web. 03 Aug. 2012. <http://www.yarr.org.uk/talk/>.

Sharp, Anne Wallace. Daring Pirate Women. Minneapolis: Lerner Publications, 2002. Print.

Smith, Rod, ed. "Traditional Sea Shanties & Sea Songs Abel Brown, the Sailor." The Traditional Music Library. N.p., n.d. Web. 03 Aug. 2012. <http://www.traditionalmusic.co.uk/sea-shanty/Abel_Brown_the_Sailor.htm>.

Smyth, William Henry. The Sailor's Word-Book. Ed. Edward Belcher. Glasgow: Blackie and Son, 1867. Project Gutenberg. Web. 04 Aug. 2012.
<http://www.gutenberg.org/files/26000/26000-0.txt>.

Summers, Mark, and John Baur. "Why talk like a pirate - and how." The Official Website for International Talk Like a Pirate Day. N.p., n.d. Web. 03 Aug. 2012. <http://www.talklikeapirate.com/>.

For more information

For more information about pirates, to learn more about talking like a pirate, pirate history, pirate shanties, and authentic pirate costume ideas, visit our website, TalkLikeAPirate.org.

Also, remember that we've created a Kindle version of this book. It can be loaned to others with Kindle readers. (Visit Amazon.com to learn how.) We've authorized it. In fact, we encourage it!

Published by Pirates Books
http://PiratesBooks.com
A division of New Forest Books
Concord, New Hampshire, USA